Patriots of the Sea Lighthouse Legacies

By
William O. Thomson

Edited by
William M. Thomson

Oil Paintings by
Ron Goyette

Copyright 2002
ISBN 09652055-7-6

Distributed by
'Scapes Me
135 Alewive Road
Kennebunk, ME 04043

Special Thanks To: Andy Andrews
Kathleen Finnegan
Ron Goyette
Timothy E. Harrison
William Heitz
Roy Salls
Connie Small
Courtney Thompson
Andrew Thomson
Kittery Historical and
Naval Museum
U.S. Coast Guard

Photo by William M.Thomson

～ Table of Contents ～

Foreword...5

Patriotic Privateers...7

The *Hannah*...12

Jonathan Haraden...15

Captain James Mugford..18

Robert Wormstead...21

Gloucester..23

Beverly..28

Salem...32

American Heritage...40

Colonial Lighthouses...42

Boston Light...45

The Revolution and Boston Light..46

The Revolution and Porstsmouth Light..................................47

The Revolution and Thachers Island Light..............................50

Lighthouses and the War of 1812...52

Chesapeake and Shannon...52

Casco Bay..54

Scituate Light...54

Bakers Island..56

Wives and Families of the Lights...59

Abbie Burgess...62

Maria Bray..66

Ida Lewis..67

Connie Small...71

West Quoddy Light..74

Petit Manan Light..74

Bass Harbor Light..76

Owls Head Light..76

Pemaquid Point Light...78

~ Table of Contents ~

(Continued)

Ram Island Light...79
Matinicus Rock Light...80
Seguin Island Light...81
Portland Head Light..82
Ram Island Ledge Light...84
Boon Island Light...85
Cape Neddick "Nubble" Light..88
The Lighthouse Legacy..92

Foreword

$\mathcal{M}$uch of America's history, like the country itself, was created by common everyday people who faced challenges with courage, strength and dedication. New England, with its vast coastline and abundant resources, was where many of these early settlers chose to live. Miles of rugged peninsulas, pounded for centuries by violent seas, and clusters of sheltered inlets and safe harbors offered access to a vast supply of fish. Just inland, deep tall forests provided significant quantities of lumber. The sea was a natural highway for transporting these commodities to the world market and returning ships brought back goods needed by the New Englanders. As this commerce grew, more people depended upon the ocean for their livelihood and the men, women, and children who worked and lived in these early days were forever tested by the natural power of the sea.

Fascinating stories have been written and told about the constant challenges faced by these people as they went about their daily lives and over the years, legend and history have become intertwined. These ordinary citizens fought hard for their independence, struggled to provide for their families, faced adversity from a harsh environment, and built a country that thrives today. From the early merchants and privateers who created the first American Navy, to the lighthouse keepers and their families who maintained a constant vigil along the shore, their stories are about hard work, responsibility and dedication to duty. These are the stories about the patriots of the sea.

Patriots of the Sea

Detail From an Oil Painting by Ron Goyette

Patriotic Privateers

In 1775 when the American seaboard colonists found themselves at war with England, they began to fit out vessels at private expense. Many of these ships later became the American Navy with a mission to harass English shipping. It is well to remember that at this time in history, the English were undisputed masters of the sea. Having just completed a successful war against France, England could now direct the full force of her energies against the colonies.

From every seaport town in the Massachusetts Bay area, large English vessels could be seen sailing up and down the coast. British warships sailed in and out of any port at will, transporting supplies without challenge. All the while, American seamen were being impressed into the British Navy. The colonists soon felt that they were in a life or death struggle, and knew that the English Navy had to be stopped. But how? Their navy, consisting of one ship, the *Hannah*, sailing out of Marblehead and Beverly, posed no threat to the British. Something else had to be done!

On June 7, 1775, the Continental Congress devised a plan that gave rise to the American privateer. Congress authorized private ships to be fitted out at private expense, for the purpose of capturing British ships, or any other vessels which in any way aided the enemy. Ships owned, outfitted and manned by civilians were commissioned by the Colonial Government. Any vessel captured by these private ships became the sole property of the owners and crew of the ship making the capture. Spoils, including the cargo and the ship itself, could be sold at any friendly port. Most often, the owners and the captain received half of the bounty and the other half was divided between the rest of the crew.

With the dream of spoils and reward money, the men set out to sea to seek their fortunes. Some succeeded and became wealthy after just one or two highly profitable voyages. These were dangerous times, and crews of the privateers tended to live life at a hard and reckless pace. Small fortunes were liquidated at the local taverns or pubs in a few short days, but they could be replaced just as quickly by shipping out on the next lucky voyage.

Privateers became very active as the war progressed and on April 3, 1776, the Continental Congress set up rules of conduct for the commanders of vessels of war and private ships which were commissioned as privateers. These eleven laws or "Instructions" were signed by John Hancock, President of Congress. If any of these laws were broken, the privateer could lose its commission and the captain and crew might be liable for any damage they caused. The ships' owners posted bonds in order to guarantee that their crews would adhere to the regulations. If the captain and his crew did not conduct themselves according to the prescribed laws, the bonds were forfeited.

Prize courts were set up in various districts to rule on the legality of the prizes and to hear disputes and charges brought against an authorized ship. The towns of the North Shore fell under the jurisdiction of the Middle District which included Boston, Salem and Newburyport. Timothy Pickering of Salem was appointed judge of this district. The Cape Cod area comprised the Southern District, while the Northern District included part of what is now Maine (Portland and Wiscasset). A privateer brought its prize into a designated harbor and after the court ruled that none of the laws had been broken, they were awarded their prize which they sold as fast as possible. The total amount of cash was distributed according to shares determined by prior agreements between the owners, captain and crew.

Other financial arrangements were made in advance by the owners and the crew. For example, the first man to sight a ship which was ultimately captured and became a prize might receive a double share of the prize money. Other brave actions which might earn an extra share were to be the first man to board an enemy ship before the capture, or to board a ship in battle. These actions required great skill and courage and men lost hands, limbs and their lives attempting to get up and over the enemy ship's gunwale.

The privateers from the North Shore were among the best in the country. One hundred and ninety-six ships sailed as privateers in the Revolution from just the port of Salem. They fought the British in all of the major sea lanes. The majority of captures were made off the coasts of Great Britain, Ireland, the West Indies and Canada. One third of all of the American privateer ships that sailed never returned. They were either captured or destroyed by the enemy.

When a new crew was forming, a recruiting officer appeared to make the announcement, backed by a fife and drum

Oil Painting by Ron Goyette

corps. He spoke only in positives, offering a chance for the common seaman to achieve glory and wealth in a few short weeks. Men were eager to sign up, and often an entire crew was enlisted in one day. Some of the recruits were experienced seamen who were unemployed and needed cash. Others were sons who had seen their fathers' businesses nearly ruined by the war. These young men hated the British Restrictive Acts of the 1760's for the monetary losses caused to their families. After the ship's company was complete, the men proceeded to the nearest tavern to drink toasts in anticipation of the great wealth and glory they were sure they would share.

Another real and very certain advantage for becoming a privateer was the food. Their fare included bread, salt beef or salt pork, rice, rum, peas, beans, potatoes, fish, turnips, butter and vinegar. All in all, food was a very strong incentive, for the privateers were fed better than the land soldiers or the sailors on the Continental ships.

The Congress also offered a small monetary advance for enlistments, equal to the pay given to the continental army men. Able bodied seamen could get an advance on their anticipated shares, of up to forty dollars. Ordinary seamen or landsmen received up to twenty dollars. These amounts were later deducted from their prize money.

The ship's company was comprised of the captain; a first lieutenant and second lieutenant; a master and master's mate; a cook; gunners; mariners and prize crews. Sailmakers were on hand to keep the sails in good repair; a blacksmith maintained the guns and weapons. The captain was in total command, his authority was unquestioned. The prize crews worked on the ship until they took control of a captured vessel and sailed it to the nearest friendly port.

After the crew reported for duty, they learned to work the ship within the harbor. Most of the crew was comprised of experienced seamen who were familiar with the sea and could handle a ship. Some were landsmen or just ordinary soldiers, and had to learn their duties from the experienced hands. Once they could successfully perform their duties, they were ready for the enemy. Because the British had every major harbor on the eastern coast blockaded, the privateers slipped out of their harbors during periods of thick fog or on particularly dark nights. It is a tribute to their dedication that they could manage to get to sea. The British ships that maintained the blockade were considerably larger than the privateers, were more heavily armed, and had better trained and more experienced seamen.

Each British frigate also had a fleet of longboats and barges that were capable of chasing the smaller and faster American ships into narrow bays, unmarked harbors or rivers. The barges carried armed marines and one or two small cannons. Pursuing the smaller ships where the frigate could not go, they often caused the privateer to run aground in shallow waters. If the local colonial militia had seen the plight of the privateer they might have attempted a rescue, firing their muskets at the barge to force its retreat to the mother ship. If not, the crew might be lucky and avoid capture by scrambling to shore where they would watch the British troops loot and then burn the grounded ship.

The ships' guns were identified by the weight of the shot they fired. A "4-pounder" fired a mortar ball that weighed four pounds. Cannons were stationary and relied on the maneuvers of the ship for their accuracy. These guns were most effective in broadside attacks. The ships also carried swivel guns. These were small but could maneuver into different positions to maintain a constant fire.

Although the opportunities for wealth and glory were many, the dangers involved in privateering were great. When the privateers stormed the decks of an opposing ship, anything at hand became a weapon. Crewmen used muskets, swords, knives, axes, pistols, iron hooks, claws, grappling hooks, and pikes to inflict damage upon the enemy. The hand-to-hand combat that ensued was merciless and many crew members lost hands, arms, legs and eyes in the battle.

Privateering was a mix of patriotism and gambling. Owners of the ships were patriotic in fitting them out, but they were gambling that they would gain financial reward. Unemployed seamen found work, but they gambled that they would return safely to shore. The owners and the crew members were all speculating on success for personal gain and glory, while still showing pride in their new country.

New England's First Continental Privateer – The *Hannah*

George Washington arrived at Cambridge, Massachusetts on July 3, 1775 to take command of the New England Army. He discovered that he could easily prevent supplies from reaching the British forces in Boston by land. However, he had no ships blockading Boston Harbor and a steady stream of British supply ships sailed in and out of the harbor at will. After consulting with John Manley of Marblehead, and with the full approval of Congress, Washington decided to arm several merchant ships to halt the flow of British supplies by sea. He appointed Colonel John Glover of Marblehead, commander of the Twenty-first Regiment, to oversee the project. This was a logical choice, for Glover had been a seafaring man for years and was also a successful ship owner. One of his ships, the schooner *Hannah*, named for his wife, was the first merchant ship to be converted.

Captain Nicholas Broughton, also of Marblehead, was appointed by Glover to take command of the ship and oversee the conversion operations. Glover owned a wharf, warehouse and cooperage in Beverly, and it was there that the *Hannah* was converted and commissioned. Since the *Hannah* was registered in Marblehead, and manned by Marblehead men, both Marblehead and Beverly claim the distinction of being the Birthplace of the United States Navy. Probably as interesting as the quarrel, is the position, or lack of it, taken by the Navy. Spokesmen for that branch of the service state that four other places (Fort Ticonderoga, NY; Crown Point, NY; Machias, ME; and Newport, RI) have equally valid claims to this honor, and they diplomatically refuse to recognize any of the claims over the others.

The *Hannah* was commissioned on September 5, 1775. She carried four 4-pounders, twelve swivel guns and a crew of fifty men. The entire crew, all Marbleheaders who had served in the Twenty-first Regiment, was hand-picked for this duty by Glover and Broughton. John Glover, Jr. and John Devereaux, Broughton's son-in-law, served as First Lieutenants.

Under the Agreement signed by General Washington, the crew was to receive one third of the sale price of all non-military cargos they captured. This did not include the recapture of American ships which were to be returned intact to their rightful owners. Because the Continental Army was in desperate need of military supplies, Washington instructed Broughton to avoid risking the *Hannah* in battles with British warships. Instead, he was to concentrate on capturing small supply ships, and waste no time before sending his prizes to Washington's headquarters in Cambridge.

Broughton sailed that same day, and his first day at sea was a near disaster. Just as he cleared the harbor, he was pursued by a British warship which forced him to race to the safety of Gloucester under full sail to evade capture. When he was certain the warship had sailed away, Broughton again put out to sea.

Within hours he captured the *Unity*, a merchant ship flying the British flag and carrying a cargo of supplies and munitions. The men were overjoyed by their good fortune but when they reached Gloucester, they found that she was an American ship captured a few days earlier by the British. When told that there would be no prize money, the men refused to return to the *Hannah*. Broughton placed them all under arrest. They were taken to Cambridge and tried by a military court. Strangely enough, the men were treated leniently. All charges were dismissed against most of them, a few were fined, and only one man was whipped and dismissed from the service. Since the *Hannah* was attached to the New England Army, the Navy does not officially recognize the men's action as mutiny. According to the Navy, the only mutiny ever attempted in U. S. Naval history occurred on the brig *Somers* in 1842.

Broughton and Glover chose a new crew and once again the *Hannah* set sail out of Beverly. She captured several more cargo vessels before running afoul of the sixteen-ton British warship *Nautilus*. With the British warship in hot pursuit, the *Hannah* succeeded in making Beverly Harbor, but the *Nautilus* was close on her stern. The ensuing battle alerted the Salem militia, which appeared on the opposite bank and caught the *Nautilus* in crossfire. The British ship was in a dangerous predicament. Since the tide was on the ebb, she could not flee to the safety of the open sea. She was canting so much that her guns could not be trained on either shore. Although her crew remained below decks as much as possible, they suffered extensive casualties. As soon as the tide came in, the *Nautilus* fled to Boston for repairs.

When George Washington learned of this action, he designated Beverly as an accredited prize port and sent troops to

Oil Painting by Ron Goyette

occupy a fort at the entrance to Beverly Harbor. Glover's Regiment was transferred to Beverly, where it remained until July, 1776 when it was reassigned. During these months, the town of Beverly supplied twenty-four men as lookouts. For twenty-four hours a day, every day, they kept a watchful eye for British warships.

In November, 1775, the *Hannah* was given a change of duty. She was much too slow for blockade duty, even with her light armament. Washington, feeling that it would be only a matter of time before she was captured, assigned her to the delivery of messages along the coast and to Europe. By this time, a number of larger and faster ships had been converted and they were being used to blockade Boston Harbor. The *Hancock* and the *Lee* were part of the fleet that took over the work that the *Hannah* had once done alone.

onathan Haraden

The life of Jonathan Haraden spanned fifty-eight years of which almost forty-seven were spent at sea. Born in 1745 in the seaport town of Gloucester, Massachusetts he spent the days of his youth listening to tales told by the Gloucester fishermen. Their yarns were extremely anti-English. The town had lost several ships to the French and English in the war of 1756, and many Gloucester seamen had been victims of English impressment. It is only natural that Jonathan, as a young boy, was strongly influenced by this anti-English fervor. Dreams of total secession were kindled within him, and constantly stoked.

In his visits with these seamen, Jonathan learned several ballads of sea adventures. He heard countless tales of smuggling, pirates, and English tyranny. All the while he was swept up in the excitement of the ships entering and leaving the harbor. The warehouses and docks were filled with molasses, rum, and all types of fish, packed in barrels and salted down, ready to be loaded aboard a ship for delivery to some foreign port. He watched cargos of wheat, tobacco, meats, iron goods, dishes and trinkets being unloaded. The lure of the sea was strong, and when he was still in his early teens he shipped out on a fishing vessel. By the time the Revolutionary War broke out, he was only thirty years old and had attained the rank of captain for the firm of Lee and Cabot of Beverly.

At the start of the war, Haraden signed on with the Massachusetts warship *Tyrannicide*. He served brilliantly as first lieutenant and was quickly promoted to captain. In command of his own ship, he sailed across the Atlantic to harass and capture British transports along the English and French coasts. In the short span of one week, he sent two large British transports to Salem with prize crews aboard. Next, he set sail for Nova Scotia, and made several captures of English fishing vessels and destroyed a good part of the Nova Scotia fishing fleet. After a brief period of sailing along the colonial coastline with little success, he set out for the West Indies where he captured three ships within a week, then headed back to Boston.

Haraden's next command was the one hundred and forty-ton *General Pickering*, a fully rigged ship commissioned by the Congress as a Letter of Marque. She carried fourteen 6-pound cannons and a crew of forty-five. Haraden set out to sea in October of 1779, and in the next two months captured an eight gun sloop, a fourteen gun full rigger and a twelve gun brig. He captured a total of thirty-four guns and delivered them to Salem Harbor. The crew received its prize money, a new crew was signed on and drilled in its duties, and in March, the *General Pickering* set sail for Bilbao, Spain with a cargo of sugar.

On the fourth day at sea, Captain Haraden came upon a British frigate carrying twenty guns. He maneuvered his ship into position and fired a broadside. The British ship, although severely damaged, returned the fire. The fight continued for an hour and a half, until the British frigate fled. The *General Pickering*, loaded down with sugar and lying low in the water, was unable to pursue the faster British ship. The cruise continued routinely, until Haraden reached the entrance to the Bay of Biscay.

At dusk the *Pickering* watch called out that a British transport ship was abeam and to the starboard. Captain Haraden delayed his approach until after dark, and then set all sails to overtake her. He had his men extend long poles, each with a small oil lamp burning at the end, from the bow and stern of the ship to make the ship appear much larger. When he was alongside the transport he hailed her, shouting that he would blow her up if she did not strike her colors at once. In the night darkness, the captain of the transport, the twenty-two gun *Golden Eagle* carrying a crew of sixty-five, could not estimate the size of the *Pickering*. He struck his colors. The deception worked, and Haraden had his first prize of the cruise.

The *Golden Eagle's* captain and part of the crew were brought aboard the *General Pickering* as prisoners, while the rest of the crew was locked in the hold of the captured ship. A prizemaster took charge of the *Golden Eagle*, and with a crew of fifteen men, set sail for Bilbao.

About three hours later, Haraden's watch sighted a large sail just over the horizon. Unfortunately, it was the *Achilles*, a British privateer carrying over one hundred and fifty men and forty-two guns. With two quick cannon blasts and some musket fire, the *Golden Eagle* was back in British possession. Haraden knew the *Pickering* would come under attack from the *Achilles*, so he sailed his much smaller ship toward the Spanish shore. He positioned her so the British ship would be exposed to broadsides when it sailed in to attack him. The tactic worked.

The battle was fierce, and although the deck of their ship was covered with blood, the American sailors remained at their guns. This was a tribute to Captain Haraden, who inspired such faith in his men. After three hours of violent exchange, the English captain withdrew. The *General Pickering* lay so low in the water that she made a poor target, while the *Achilles* was so huge that

Oil Painting by Ron Goyette

17

the American gunners seemed to hit her at will. Haraden could see how badly the British ship was damaged and he set out after her, but damage to his own ship prevented him from overtaking the British frigate. Nine men lay dead on the *Pickering*. Her rigging was in tatters; fragments of wood, masts, spars, lines, gear and sails were scattered over her deck. Haraden managed to recapture the *Golden Eagle* however, and sailed it into Bilbao Harbor. After enjoying a well deserved celebration, he sold his own cargo, and the prize ship and its cargo as well. His ship was repaired and he headed back out to sea.

Stories of Haraden's exploits are plentiful. Once, when he was being chased by a British man-of-war the wind died down. He ordered his men into the long boats and they rowed his ship out of the range of the British guns. Another time he took on three British ships at once - his attack pattern was such that the British were forced to fight him one at a time and he captured all three ships. He made several captures by disguising his ship as a slow unarmed transport. In another engagement, after a six hour battle, Haraden withdrew to repair his ship and then returned to force his adversary to surrender. His name was known throughout the British Navy, and he was respected as a fearless adversary.

The last years of Captain Jonathan Haraden's life were spent in ill health; the sea had taken its toll. He died in 1803 in his brick house on Essex Street in Salem.

Captain James Mugford

James Mugford served as paymaster with the Twenty-first Massachusetts Regiment during the first months of the war. Early in May, 1776 he was captured by a British impressment crew and taken aboard the *Lively*, a twenty gun British warship engaged in blockading north shore ports. Mugford had recently married a young lady from Marblehead. When she learned of his capture, she rowed out to the *Lively* to bargain for her husband's freedom.

So impressed was the British captain with her courage that he immediately set Mugford free.

While on the *Lively*, Mugford gained some valuable information. From discussions he had overheard and documents he had seen, he learned that a number of British supply ships carrying weapons would soon arrive in Boston. These weapons were desperately needed by the American forces. He set out to inform Archibald Selman, owner of the *Franklin*, a large schooner. Within two days, the *Franklin* was ready to sail. Meanwhile, General Glover signed the necessary papers commissioning the schooner as a privateer and assigned her to Washington's North Shore Fleet. James Mugford was named captain of the *Franklin*, which carried four 4-pound cannons, two swivel guns and a crew of twenty. The men were well armed with muskets, knives, hooks, pikes, pistols, clubs and other small weapons.

Mugford's first problem was to evade the ever present British ships blockading the harbor. He accomplished this by sailing out during the night. The following morning he sighted the British supply ship *Hope*, one of the ships he had seen mentioned in the documents. He set all sails, and when he was close to the ship he fired a broadside. The *Hope* quickly hove to and struck her colors. Mugford put a prize crew aboard her and the two ships headed for Shirley Gut, a channel running between Deer Island and Winthrop, Massachusetts.

Just outside the entrance to the channel, the *Hope* ran aground on a shoal called Faun Bar. As Mugford was trying to determine a way to refloat the *Hope*, a British warship sailed into view. It was apparent that her captain was unfamiliar with these waters, for he decided to wait until the tide re-floated the ship before he attempted to recapture it.

Mugford seized upon the opportunity to buy time and he set all sails on the *Franklin* and raced to Revere to seek help. The response was overwhelming. A small group of volunteers sailed some longboats over to the *Hope* while a large group of men marched overland to Winthrop. They unloaded the ship's cargo into the small boats. The bounty included twelve hundred muskets (complete with bayonets), powder, shells, three mortars and several cannons, all of which were immediately dispatched to Washington's army. Relieved of her cargo, the *Hope* floated free of the shoal, and was sailed into Lynn by the prize crew.

Two days later, Mugford slipped out of Marblehead Harbor to search for more of the supply ships. Once again, Faun Bar caused him trouble. As he sailed close to Winthrop, his own ship ran aground. Before she could be re-floated, she was spotted and recognized by several British warships. Determined to avenge the *Hope*, the British sent two hundred marines in nine longboats after Mugford. Because of its list, the *Franklin's* 4-pounders were useless, but the swivel guns were manned and ready to fire. The rest of the crew, armed with muskets, crouched low behind the gunwales.

When the longboats came within range of his guns, Mugford gave the order to fire. Although a number of their marines were killed, the British kept rowing, hoping to board the *Franklin* before her guns could be reloaded. By this time however, the tide was ebbing fast and the strong current prevented the British oarsmen from making headway. After two of their longboats were sunk and more than seventy of their men killed, the British pulled back.

The British marines had been firing at the *Franklin* in volleys and in the final exchange, Mugford was struck by a musket ball. Shouting, "Don't give up the vessel," he crumpled to the deck and died, the only casualty suffered by the *Franklin*. Although Captain James Lawrence is generally credited with saying "Don't give up the ship," Mugford's order preceded his by thirty-seven years.

Unaware that Mugford was dead, the British sailed away as soon as their longboats returned. That night, the incoming tide re-floated the *Franklin* and she sailed for Marblehead. News of the battle preceded her and a large quiet crowd was waiting when she sailed into the Harbor. Mugford was given a hero's funeral by the townspeople and he was laid to rest in the Old Burying Ground in Marblehead, where a large monument marks his final resting place.

Robert Wormstead

During the War for Independence, many private citizens performed courageous and fearless acts for their new country. Some of these people have gone unnoticed and their stories have not been told. Robert Wormstead, a private citizen of Marblehead, might well fall into this category.

He spent most of his idle hours at the Cod Tavern, which faced the ocean at the foot of Glover Lane. There were two British frigates stationed in the area and their crews frequented this pub when they were permitted to go ashore. When the sailors dropped in for a mug of grog, Robert took great delight in tormenting them. He expounded upon his patriotism and in clear explicit terms tossed out incendiary remarks to infuriate the British sailors. The result of his outbursts was always the same: Robert would be challenged to a duel.

He was a skilled fencer, and to further infuriate the British, he would arm himself with just a broomstick against the sailors' swords. He toyed with the opposition before disarming them and he sent them back to their ships with lost pride and dignity. Then, the robust Marblehead fisherman would sit back and let out hoarse, harsh roars of laughter. He was not at all concerned about promoting good Anglo-American relations.

Wormstead was in the local militia when the war broke out and he fought at Bunker Hill. He returned home to ship out on a privateer, a small sloop known as the *Freemason*, which was soon captured by a large British privateer. A prize crew boarded the ship and along with the other American prisoners, Wormstead was taken into the hold and chained to stanchions. Fencing was not his only skill however, for he was also an expert lock picker. By dusk, he had freed himself and the entire ship's company from their chains. The crew then organized a plan to retake the ship by overpowering the captain and the prize crew at the same instant. Wormstead captured the British prize captain while his shipmates overpowered the crew. The *Freemason* was back in the hands of the original crew and the British were chained in the hold.

Wormstead had a plan to go after the British privateer that had originally captured the *Freemason*. In order to conceal the fact that the patriots had retaken their ship, he directed that the British flag remain flying on the masthead. He then came up beside the British ship and the men were able to board her and claim her as their own prize.

After this action, Wormstead was assigned to command a schooner which he sailed to Nova Scotia. He captured several small fishing vessels and in one encounter, was almost taken by a British frigate. He and his crew abandoned ship and swam ashore. They hid in the woods until the British left, stole a small fishing boat, and slipped into the harbor and retook their ship after a brief struggle. Before the British on the frigate learned of his escape, Wormstead's schooner was far out to sea. Wormstead was one of the many unsung heroes of the Revolutionary War.

Oil Painting by Ron Goyette

Contributions of Gloucester

Gloucester, Massachusetts had the harbor, the location, the men and every other conceivable ingredient necessary for successful privateering. Patriotic fervor ran high in this north shore town and Gloucester's privateering record was excellent. The people carried their share of the war effort with distinction and pride, but not without a great deal of hardship and suffering. Many wives waited in vain for their husbands to return from the sea. Hundreds of children were left without fathers. Families lost their wage earners. Privateersmen returned from the sea sick and injured, too feeble to work. The strain on these men and their families was severe but their patriotism and courage was not dimmed.

When the Massachusetts Legislature passed the act of November 1, 1775 legalizing privateering, the people of Gloucester were ready. The only ships available in the harbor were small fishing boats, but with a few modifications to their decks, they were armed with small swivel guns. Three quarters of the men in this small seaport town were either fishermen or working in related jobs such as shipyard workers, repairmen, or warehouse hands. Cut off from their occupations by the war, and with the British blockading the ports, they were unable to earn a living. Poverty in the town increased and the men were left with only two choices: to enlist in the Continental Army or to ship out in a privateer. They did both, but as the war progressed, more men chose to become privateers

The first small boats sailing out of Gloucester Harbor carried crews of eight to ten men. They initially captured some small Canadian coastal schooners with cargos of fuel and livestock. The money received for these meager prizes did not fatten the purses of the sailors nor did it contribute much food to the town.

The first major tragedy involving the Gloucester men occurred in the fall of 1775. Three small fishing privateers sailing out around Rockport sighted what they thought was a large British transport. The privateers set their sails and started the chase. Soon after, another colonial ship appeared. The captain of this larger ship sailing out of Newburyport hailed the Gloucester fleet, and took aboard its combined crew of twenty men while skeleton crews sailed the three smaller vessels back to Gloucester. The Newburyport ship prepared to take the large British transport but the Americans had made a serious miscalculation. The British transport was the disguised frigate *Milford*, and when she rolled out two tiers of guns, the privateersmen knew they were doomed.

The small American ship was completely unprepared for this turn of events, and after a brief exchange of fire, she struck her colors. The crew was captured and sent to New York City where they were imprisoned in an old ship's hull known as the "floating pest house." The stench alone was unbearable, and the dark, filthy stalls between decks were breeding grounds for disease and plague. The men were kept in the hull at night, and forced to work loading supplies during the day. The punishment for being a privateersman was harsh - the men were constantly whipped and flogged by the British Redcoats.

Throughout their imprisonment the crew stayed together. Later, they succeeded in stealing a small British barge and they were able to row safely to the New Jersey shore. They slowly made their way back to Gloucester. One of the men had been killed and one had been wounded; another crewmember had lost his hand. The all suffered from malnutrition, smallpox and torn limbs. When they arrived back in Gloucester, they were nursed back to health, and most of them returned to privateering. Their experiences taught them that it was far more desirable to die at sea than to be sent to a prison ship.

The Gloucester privateers earned more money than the Continental Soldiers, especially if their ship was successful in its captures. In many cases, extra pay was given to the injured to compensate for the loss of eyes or limbs. On the other hand, any man who deserted his ship forfeited his share of the prize money. Against great odds, this tiny fishing fleet of Gloucester made a courageous start at privateering. Soon they would have more large ships in their fleet and more valuable prizes to their credit.

The first large ship to sail out of Gloucester was the former cargo ship *Britannia*. Its name was immediately changed to the *Warren*, in honor of General Warren, killed at the battle of Bunker Hill. William Coas was captain and she carried eight guns. On her first venture out to sea the Warren brought in three prizes: the *Picary*, a ship of four hundred tons; a smaller vessel; and the ship *Sarah and Elizabeth*. This third capture was, without doubt, one of the most humorous in the history of privateering.

The British captain, William Foot, commanded the large ship of five hundred tons which carried a valuable cargo of cash, sugar, rum, cotton, indigo and mahogany. His wife and a few of her lady friends were passengers. The ship had departed from Jamaica a few days earlier and was sailing toward London. At almost noon, Captain Coas of the *Warren* sighted the *Sarah and Elizabeth's* topsail over the horizon. He kept his small ship out of sight until dusk and then set all sails to overtake the British ship.

During the darkest part of the night Coas sailed up alongside the ship and called out to Captain Foot to strike his colors or be sunk with a broadside. The captain's wife and her lady friends were seized by panic. They had heard dreadful stories about the patriots and feared that if their ship resisted, they would be scalped or fed to the sharks for entertainment. They started to weep and in a short time, became hysterical. Captain Foot allowed himself to be persuaded by the ladies actions, and surrendered his ship without firing a shot.

At dawn Captain Foot saw his captors clearly for the first time. The sight of the tiny American craft with its eight puny guns filled him with humiliation. Needless to say, he felt no great affection for his wife and her lady friends. Foot remained below decks as John Somes, the prize master, brought the ship into Gloucester Harbor. He stayed in Gloucester and within a year he had made arrangements to purchase the *Sarah and Elizabeth*. Just before he set sail, Captain Foot received news of the final fate of the *Warren*. On her third cruise, under the command of Captain Silas Howell, she was captured after three days at sea. The ship was sent to New York, and its crew was imprisoned.

At another time, the Gloucester vessel the *Langdon* was leaving the harbor and the captain decided to fire off one of the 6-pounders as a salute. This was a direct violation of privateering law, as all powder was supposed to be conserved and used only in battle. Nevertheless, the captain fired the salute. The gun blew up and injured four crewmen. This was the end of the cruise for the *Langdon*.

One of the largest ships to sail out of the harbor was the brig *Gloucester*. She carried eighteen guns and a crew of one hundred and thirty men. On her first cruise she made two quick captures, the British ships *Spark* and *Two Friends* which were sent in as prizes. Then she vanished! The *Gloucester* completely disappeared and no one knew her fate. No word was ever received about any member of her crew. Nineteen men serving on the ship as part of its crew were from the small town of Manchester, Massachusetts and the loss of the *Gloucester* was a tremendous blow to that town.

One of the men, Dr. Joseph Whipple, left his wife and seven children behind. Half of all the crew members on the ship were married and averaged three children per family. The loss of this ship left many fatherless children. Legend has it that at about the same time the ship disappeared, a large mysterious body of light appeared briefly over the house of each crew member. The townspeople thought this was a vague supernatural message.

David Pearce was almost forced into bankruptcy when his ship the *Gloucester* disappeared. He financed another ship however, the *General Starks* and fared much better. This ship made three small captures and then set sail for Bilbao where the crew came down with yellow fever. They were forced to remain in the harbor for three weeks until there were enough healthy men to set sail. On her way back to Gloucester she captured two large British transports and these prizes more than paid for the cost of the ship and the voyage.

The following winter was so cold that the *General Starks* was frozen in Gloucester Harbor. She sailed out with the spring thaw and brought in three more prizes in as many weeks. On her next cruise, the *Starks* was captured by the British ship *Chatham*.

Her captain and crew were taken to the British prison in Halifax. Sometime later, they were involved in a prisoner exchange and boarded a sloop headed to Boston. They never reached the port. It is believed that all men were lost when the sloop was sunk in a storm.

British warships were not the only peril the privateers faced. During one voyage two privateers, the *Tempest* and the *Polly* were sailing together when they ran into a storm. The crew of the *Polly* watched in horror as the *Tempest* was struck by lightning and the ship virtually disintegrated. All hands on the *Tempest* were lost. The crew of the *Polly* had the terrible task of bringing home the sad news of the disaster to the families and friends of the crew.

Occasionally a problem would arise between privateers that would have to be settled in the prize court. One such problem, or difference of opinion, involved the *Harlequin* of Gloucester and the *Wasp* of Salem. They were cruising along the same course,

Oil Painting by Ron Goyette

and at approximately the same time, they both sighted a British rum ship. Few seamen would turn down the chance to capture some prize rum, and both ships made chase. The *Wasp* turned the British ship into the path of the *Harlequin* which called for the

27

British ship to strike its colors. The crew of the *Wasp* felt that their part in the capture had earned them a share of the prize, but those on the *Harlequin* did not see it that way. The owners of the *Wasp* took the case to the prize court and the judge decided that an equal distribution should be made between the two ships. It was later reported, but not authenticated, that three hogsheads of the prize rum were given to the lawyer and the judge as a "donation" from the crew of the *Wasp*.

As time passed, Gloucester sent several more ships to sea and they continued to distinguish themselves in the same manner as the ships that sailed earlier. Their crews fought as hard, and with the same spirit of loyalty and drive that was characteristic of all Gloucester seamen. By the time the war ended, the town had lost almost one third of its male population and was on the brink of financial ruin. The people had suffered and were in need of all types of supplies. Food, clothing and most of life's essentials were extremely scarce. Nevertheless, the proud citizens worked hard to rebuild the town. They were content in the knowledge that they had earned every bit of freedom that was the foundation of their new country.

Privateering in Beverly

Beverly Harbor is situated about one mile north of Salem Harbor. Because of their close proximity to one another they are considered sister ports. During Revolutionary times both ports were under the jurisdiction of a single naval officer and oftentimes one port would receive credit for the action of a ship registered from the other port. Many Beverly merchants were active in privateering. The Cabots, the Browns, the Himans, the Lovetts, the Thorndikes and the Lees all financed ships. Beverly can also boast of many successful commanders such as Hill, Giles, Smith and Little.

Beverly's privateer history began with the *Hannah*, as described earlier. Several small continental ships followed soon after. Receiving their commissions in Beverly were the *Lynch*, the *Franklin*, the *Lee* and the *Hancock*. The presence of these government owned ships made Beverly a very important harbor. Since most of their captures were brought into Beverly, the town had to construct new wharfs and docks further up the river to accommodate them.

During this period the Continental Army under General Washington was encamped at Dorchester Heights, overlooking Boston, which was still occupied by the British. Beverly served an important function in the opening stages of the Revolution as a source for the Army's much needed supplies. Weapons, clothing and food captured by the privateers and unloaded in Beverly were carried overland to Cambridge to aid General Washington in his campaign against the British.

Henry Knox was carrying out one of the most significant missions of the war at this time. A party under his leadership was transporting fifty-nine heavy guns over ice and snow from Fort Ticonderoga to Dorchester Heights. While Knox was performing this difficult and dangerous task, Captain John Manley, commanding the *Lee*, captured the British brigantine *Nancy*. Captain Manley lived in Marblehead and the *Lee* was a Marblehead ship, commissioned and fitted out in Beverly. These two seemingly unrelated actions, taking place hundreds of miles apart, proved to be a very lucky coincidence.

Along with an abundant supply of musket balls and muskets, the holds of the captured brigantine *Nancy* were loaded with four and six pound artillery balls. The captured artillery balls were the exact size needed for the heavy guns brought in by Henry Knox from Ticonderoga. Upon seeing the cannon, the British General William Howe realized that he had been outmaneuvered and on March 17, 1776 he ordered the evacuation of thirteen thousand British troops from Boston and sailed his army to Halifax.

As the war continued, more private ships were commissioned in Beverly and at least two ships per week were sailing out of the harbor. On her first cruise, the ten gun brig *Retaliation* commanded by Captain Eleayer Giles captured four ships bound from Jamaica to London. They totaled over one thousand tons. Giles continued to sail and was subsequently wounded, lost an eye, and was eventually captured. He was the first Beverly captain sent to the Halifax prison.

Other Beverly captains kept pressuring the British. Captain Benjamin Smith, sailing around the West Indies, sent back several prizes. Captain John Little had numerous engagements with the British and once fought two British ships simultaneously. When his crew started to panic as their ship was hit by volley after volley, Captain Little drew his sword and threatened to personally run it through the stomach of any man who deserted his post. The crew rallied and the battle continued to rage for three hours, until the British withdrew.

The name of Captain Hugh Hill topped the British Navy's most wanted list. Hill brought more captured vessels into the port of Beverly than any other Beverly captain. His reputation was that of a kind and gentle officer who was fair and benevolent to both crew and captives. He was known on occasion to release prisoners in neutral ports rather than have them imprisoned. He was highly distinguished for his bravery and expert navigating skills.

Hill was a superb strategist and had a keen sense of timing about when to maneuver, attack and board a ship. While sailing the *Pilgrim* off the coast of Ireland he sighted a British warship, but did not consider conditions favorable to engage her. Instead, he ran up the British flag and played the part of a British privateer. The other captain brought his ship to within a few yards of the *Pilgrim* and called out that he was on the lookout for Captain Hugh Hill of Beverly, the widely known privateer. Hill answered that he too, was looking for him. The next morning, when wind conditions were more favorable, Hill ran up the American flag and attacked the British warship. The British captain struck his colors and was astonished to discover that he had been taken by Hugh Hill. Hill gained fame commanding the *Pilgrim* and later the *Cicero*.

Another ship sailing out of Beverly Harbor was the *Terrible Creature*. Owned by John and Andrew Cabot she carried over one hundred men and sixteen guns. While sailing outside of

30

Bilbao under the command of Nathaniel West, she ran into a small fleet of British transports and captured the entire fleet. The *Terrible Creature* had made so many captures that not only her prize crew, but most of her main crew had to sail in captured ships. West was compelled to return to Beverly to enlist more men so his ship could continue her voyage and bring the rest of her captures in safely.

One of the largest privateers to sail out of Beverly was the *Black Prince*. She weighed over two hundred tons and carried eighteen guns and a company of one hundred and thirty men. After her commission, she sailed on the ill-fated Penobscot expedition and was destroyed at Castine, Maine. Her crew managed to escape and made their way back to Beverly. The *Black*

Oil Painting by Ron Goyette

Prince was owned jointly by several men. Built at a cost of about two hundred thirty-eight thousand dollars, her loss was a severe financial blow to her owners.

Privateering involved not only the capture of a ship, but often the recapture of an American vessel. The *Hope*, a small ship carrying six guns and sailing out of Beverly Harbor engaged in such an action. She was taken by the British ship *Prince Edward*

31

and a British prize crew was put aboard. Half of the *Hope's* crew remained aboard, while the other half was confined aboard the *Prince Edward*. After two days, the American crew overpowered the English crews on both ships and sailed them back to Beverly Harbor where the prize court ruled that no shares would be paid for the capture. As it turned out, the *Prince Edward* was a former Gloucester ship, the *Wilkes*. It had been captured by the British and renamed the *Prince Edward*.

Beverly claims sixty ships commissioned in its harbor and manned by Beverly crews. Two-thirds of all the men that sailed these ships spent some time in a British prison during the war. This fact alone is evidence of the hardship suffered not only by the crews that sailed, but by the families they left at home.

Salem

In the year 1775 the population of Salem was just over six thousand people, including all the sailors in port. About fifty vessels a year sailed from Salem Harbor and over one hundred ninety-six ships were commissioned there. During the Revolution, a ship considered a Salem ship was one owned by a Salem merchant, usually commanded by a Salem captain with a crew recruited from the Salem docks, and was always fitted up and made ready to sail from a Salem shipyard. The commission or Letter of Marque was also listed at Salem.

In some situations, two or three merchants from adjoining towns might have owned stock in one ship. Confusion concerning the port of origin also arose when ships were manned by personnel from different towns. For example, a Salem ship rigged and commissioned in Salem with a Beverly captain and owners from Danvers and Ipswich might be listed with any of the above mentioned towns as a home port.

The first privateer ship to sail out of Salem was a small schooner named the *Dolphin*. Previously she had been used as a coastal schooner, sailing between towns along the coast transporting small cargos from warehouse to warehouse. The ship was classed as seventeen tons, was fitted with eight swivel guns and carried a crew of twenty-five men. After the crew went through a short training period, the Dolphin set out on her first cruise.

The skipper of the *Dolphin* was Richard Masury, a very capable seaman with twenty years of experience at sea. He proved his skill on the first voyage when the schooner captured three prizes which netted each crewman about two hundred and fifty dollars. This was considered to be a very fine year's pay per man. The owners and the captain divided up the equivalent of approximately six thousand two hundred and fifty dollars.

Elias Hasket Derby, America's first millionaire, was very active in privateering. His schooner the *Sturdy Beggar* and the sloop *Revenge* were fitted out and made ready for action. The crews were assembled and drilled and made ready to sail. On the evening before their departure, they celebrated their forthcoming cruise at the local tavern, devouring large quantities of grog and food. They were a strapping group of seamen, and must have appeared monstrous to the young boys who peered into the taverns and hid along the docks watching them in action. The *Sturdy Beggar* carried eight guns and a crew of thirty-five men; the *Revenge* carried ten guns and a crew of forty men. These tiny Salem ships had to sail through the British blockade, manned by the British frigate *Milford*, one of a fleet of eleven powerful enemy ships that sailed in and out of the harbors between Providence, Rhode Island and Wiscasset, Maine.

Because captured English prize ships were sailed into the colonial harbors where the prize courts were located, the British deployed their naval ships as close to prize ships as possible, in order to intercept and recapture them. The colonists, however, successfully captured such a large number of prize ships that the British were forced to decide to either intensify the blockade, or send the larger frigates with the transports as escorts. Since the colonial privateers were making captures all along the eastern seaboard, as well as off European, Middle Eastern and Caribbean ports, the British chose the latter alternative and were forced to escort their vessels. This weakened the blockade and afforded the colonial privateers greater freedom in sailing in and out of their home ports.

Salem Harbor bustled with activity as the war continued. Ships were constructed rapidly, and a huge labor pool was centered in the port. The booming sounds of hammers and the cracking sounds of axes filled the air. The town smelled of fresh cut wood, of tar, and of pitch. The workers, the merchants and the naval architects were all very busy, suggesting changes to improve the size and speed of the vessels. Almost all of the ships were constructed of wood, and each piece had to be hand worked. Massive timbers were used to put these ships together to prevent them from cracking under their heavy loads. Heavier ships required more sails to attain a favorable speed. Aside from the hauling of heavy timber, which was done by horses, the only other source of power used to construct the ships was the exhausting, back-breaking labor of men.

Each week a new or completely overhauled ship slipped into the water. With little fanfare, the yard foreman often poured a bottle of rum over the deck of the ship before it splashed into the harbor. The workers cheered and clambered aboard to complete the rigging and install the fittings. The sail makers delivered the sails, dockworkers loaded supplies and the newly enlisted crew was mustered and made ready to sail.

Cannons were secured along both sides of the ship so they could be fired when the ship was broadside. Because they were inaccurate, the more guns a ship carried, the better her chances were for a hit. Many men were required to operate the guns, which had to be hand loaded and touched off with a torch.

In addition to the gunners, a successful privateer required a boarding crew and prize crews, as well as a regular working crew. These ships required a lot more crewmembers than a regular merchant ship. For example, when outfitted as a privateer, the ship *Grand Turk* carried a crew of one hundred and twenty-five. After the war, under the command of Samuel Williams, she carried a crew of fifteen.

The *Rover*, under the command of Simon Forester, was another ship that set sail from Salem Harbor. Carrying fifty men and some very heavy arms, she became involved in an incident in which the British transport she was trying to capture blew up, killing twenty-five men aboard. Three survivors were taken on board the *Rover* and described the incident. Apparently, a hot shot fell into the powder room and detonated a barrel of black powder which blew apart the ship's hull. The *Rover* continued her cruise and captured four sloops and a brigantine which was later recaptured off Gloucester Harbor by the British ship *Milford*. Like a lot of privateering captains, who after leaving the sea went on to successful careers in politics, business and banking, Simon Forester later became one of the leading merchants in Salem.

Oil Painting by Ron Goyette

Other ships followed at a rapid pace. The *True American*, *Success*, *General Putnam*, and *Liberty* were all out looking for captures. Their names reflected the patriotic fervor of the salty, self-reliant seekers of independence that named them. These ships carried crews of fifty men each and averaged ten guns per ship. In August of 1777, Salem had over three hundred and sixty men sailing in privateers. The prizes taken that month totaled just over six thousand pounds. The prize money and prize ships coming into the port were a driving force to get more ships and crews ready for action and out to sea.

One of the largest ships launched was the very fast brigantine, *Oliver Cromwell*, owned by John Derby, the youngest son of Richard and the brother of Elias Hasket Derby. Under the command of Captain William Coles, she carried sixteen guns and a crew of one hundred and thirty-five men. The *Oliver Cromwell* was credited with seven prizes. Five were brought into Beverly Harbor and two into Bilbao, Spain. In one battle, she nearly defeated a large British warship in the English Channel, embarrassing the British commander and convincing the colonists that larger ships, heavier arms and larger crews could stand up to most British warships. Another brigantine, the *Lion*, set sail at this time under Captain Benjamin Warren. She carried over one hundred men and some heavy arms. Although not much is known of her cruises, she sailed in December and harassed the British trade routes between England and the West Indies.

A fleet of fifteen brigs were soon launched, followed by four large barques. At that time Salem had thirty armed ships at sea with over eighteen hundred men and three hundred and fifty guns. Some of the captains in command of these ships were Lander, Ropes, Woodbury, Gray, Nichols, Putnam and Felt. New financial backers were Wait, Page, Crowningshield, White and Goodale. A large part of the colonies' war at sea involved the town of Salem. Privateering had developed into a very profitable business and had become a very important industry in the town.

Privateering voyages did not always end with profit and glory; many ships never returned. Life at sea was not easy. Ships were caught in storms or hurricanes; others ran into dense fog and were smashed on rocks or reefs; some, caught in violent lightning storms, were split in two, set afire and sunk. They hit obstructions in the sea - ice or debris from the ruins of other ships lost before them. Powder rooms exploded. Crewmembers were stricken with a variety of diseases and died.

One of the worst naval disasters of the war, the Penobscot Expedition, claimed five Salem ships. In 1779 the British were occupying the town of Castine, Maine as a base from which to patrol the New England coastline. Forty ships carrying a thousand men were dispatched from Massachusetts to drive them from the area. When the fleet reached Castine, instead of quickly attacking the outnumbered British, the colonial ships sailed around in confusion, giving the British time to get reinforcements from Nova Scotia. As more English ships arrived the American fleet was trapped. Their only alternative was to head up the Penobscot River where they grounded and set fire to the fleet to avoid capture. The crews fled into the woods. One Salem vessel was captured, two were burned and two were grounded on the shoals.

Later that same year, Captain Daniel Ropes and his brig, the *Wild Cat* were captured and taken to Halifax. Ropes and his crew were treated harshly in this British prison not known for its congenial hospitality. They were confined in irons, given little food, and held in a dark cell infested with rodents. When word reached Salem of the plight of Captain Ropes and his crew, an exchange of prisoners was arranged, and the captain and crew were released.

Among the treasures the successful privateers confiscated from the ships they captured were molasses, tobacco, rum, sugar, exotic foods, ammunition, cash, wood, pipes, cotton, wine, tea, elephant tusks and gold dust. Goods that could not be purchased before the war were for sale, at inflated prices, in colonial prize ports. A significant number of the prize ships sent into Salem Harbor were converted to American privateers, replacing those lost from the American fleet.

The *Essex*, a Salem and Beverly ship under John Cathcart, sent in two ships that sold with their cargos for two hundred forty-three thousand pounds. Profits like this enticed other merchants to speculate and finance more ships and crews. By 1778, the fleet numbered sixty active ships including eight large vessels. Only three sloops remained, evidence that the concentration had shifted to power, arms, large crews, and speed. The main gun power had gone from four and six-pound guns to ten and 12-pounders.

The eighteen-gun ship *Pilgrim*, under the command of Captain Robinson, had seen action in the West Indies and was heading back to Salem when she encountered the hostile British ship *Mary*. The two ships engaged in a five and one-half hour battle. Both ships suffered damage and experienced casualties. The young gunners were close to tears as the harsh cruel realities of war were laid before them. Men were lying all about, their bodies slashed with sharp splinters and torn by flying debris and gear. The wounds were painful, severe and sometimes fatal.

The deafening blasts of the cannons were unyielding; neither side compromised and the battle continued mercilessly. Both ships were engulfed in smoke and flame. The stench of black powder permeated the air. Punctured bodies continued to fall, staining the decks with blood. Finally, the British captain was hit in the neck by a deadly shot and the *Mary* struck her colors. The victory was a costly one for Captain Robinson. Nine of his men had been killed and his ship just managed to stay afloat. A prize crew boarded the *Mary*, and the two ships headed for Salem Harbor.

Apparently the survivors of the *Mary* had not had enough action. They attacked the prize crew and tried to retake the ship. Captain Robinson, who was close by, sent aid over from the *Pilgrim* and they managed to beat off the attack. The captain's patience was exhausted but fortunately for his enemies, he was a man of benevolence when not engaged in battle. He provided the British with a compass and provisions, and set them adrift in a longboat knowing that they could make it to land. The *Pilgrim* captured nine more prizes, but no other engagement was as bloody as the one fought with the *Mary*.

In 1781 Admiral George Rodney of the British Navy captured the seaport town of St. Eustatia in the Dutch West Indies. This small port had been a haven for the colonial privateers. Captain Jonathan Haraden was in the harbor at the time, aboard his famous ship the *General Pickering*. He fell into the hands of the British but managed to escape, and was given command of a new ship, the *Julius Caesar*. With his new command, he continued to chase and capture the British with the same brilliance and fervor as he did when he commanded the *General Pickering*.

By the year 1782, the war was beginning to favor the colonies. The conflict on the seas was being waged by much larger ships. Salem had over fifty ships in the larger class and the people of the town continued to pursue their privateering activities with great vigor. One of the last ships to sail out of Salem Harbor was the *Grand Turk*, a three hundred ton ship carrying twenty-two guns. The ship was owned by Elias Hasket Derby, who chose Thomas Simons as its captain. Measuring one hundred feet from bow to stern, she was large but fast. The ship was docked at Derby Wharf which extended almost two thousand feet out into Salem

Oil Painting by Ron Goyette

Harbor in revolutionary days, and was lined with active warehouses. Today, this wharf is one of the few pre-revolutionary wharfs still in existence. As a national historic site, it is owned by the U. S. Park Service. Directly across the street from the wharf is the home where Elias Hasket Derby lived from 1762 up through the Revolution.

Mr. Derby could stand at his window and look out at the great new ship that would soon bring him fame. The crew of one hundred and twenty men was recruited in just a few short days. Derby possessed a keen insight and selected forceful men and high quality leaders, many of whom he had known as boys and watched them grow. It was considered an honor to be in his employ, and men were proud to serve on his ships.

The *Grand Turk* sailed out as a privateer in June of 1781 and by April 1783 had made sixteen captures. The profits were shared between the owners, captain and the crew. It is not known

39

for certain how much profit the ship returned, but a fair estimate would be at least one million dollars. The ship was captained by Joseph Pratt on its second and third cruises. The prizes captured by this famous ship were a tribute to two great captains.

Conclusion - The American Heritage

Was privateering profitable? Small fortunes were made during the privateer era but fortunes were also lost. Few men became financially wealthy; most families suffered some type of loss. Crewmen were killed or injured in battle, imprisoned, left stranded on strange islands and often just disappeared, their fates unknown. Widows and orphans left behind suffered long after the war.

Throughout the seven year period of conflict, the American privateers cost the British the equivalent of ten million 1775 dollars in lost cargo and ships. They forced the British merchantmen to sail in fleets and then forced the British Navy to protect those fleets. Their victories and struggles at sea proved to be important in the development of our great country and we owe the privateers a debt of gratitude.

Wealth does not necessarily have to be measured in monetary terms. The inheritance of freedom, shared by over two hundred and seventy-five million Americans today, is surely proof of a great wealth from which we all continue to profit. Privateering made a vital contribution to the American fight for independence, and while many of its heroes will remain nameless, the results of their patriotic acts and courageous deeds will live on in the hearts of all. Privateering was profitable, indeed!

Lighthouse Legacies

Detail From an Oil Painting by Ron Goyette

Lighthouses of Colonial Times

During the colonial period, ship owners, shipbuilders and traders were among the wealthiest citizens in America. In Salem, Massachusetts Elias Haskett Derby, mentioned earlier, became America's first millionaire through his ownership of a large fleet of ships and coastal schooners. Because their survival depended upon sea trade, people recognized the need to build beacons and lighthouses to protect the important sea lanes along the shore.

The first lighthouse constructed in the United States was Boston Light (Boston, MA). Built in 1716, it was twice destroyed by the colonials and once by the British. At the time, Boston was considered a major port with as many as three hundred vessels entering its waters in a year. The light was ceded to the Federal Government in 1789 along with eleven other colonial lighthouses that became the backbone of America's lighthouse system. The other New England colonial lighthouses are Brant Point (MA) 1746; Beavertail (RI) 1749; New London Harbor (CT) 1760; Portsmouth Harbor (NH) 1771; Cape Ann (MA) 1771; Nantucket (MA) 1784; and Newburyport Harbor (MA) 1788. Also considered colonial lighthouses but built outside of New England were Sandy Hook (NJ) 1764; Cape Henlopen (DE) 1765; and Charleston Main (Morris Island, SC) 1767.

Portsmouth Harbor Light
New Hampshire
Established 1771

U.S. Coast Guard Photo

New London Harbor
Connecticut
Established 1760

U.S. Coast Guard Photo

Brant Point Light
Massachusetts
Established 1746

U.S. Coast Guard Photo

43

Beavertail Light
Rhode Island
Established 1749

U.S. Coast Guard Photo

Sandy Hook Light
New Jersey
Established 1764

U.S. Coast Guard Photo

Newburyport Harbor
Massachusetts
Established 1788

U.S. Coast Guard Photo

44

oston Light

*A*s the center of maritime history in the early eighteenth century, the entrance to Boston Harbor was a natural place to build a lighthouse. In 1715, the Boston Light Bill was passed and fourteen months later on September 14, 1716 the stone tower built on Little Brewster Island was placed into service.

Boston Light   *U.S. Coast Guard Photo*

45

George Worthylake was the first keeper of Boston Light. He was paid a salary of only fifty pounds a year, but he was allowed to earn extra income as a navigational pilot for ships sailing into the harbor. Two years and two months after taking his post, Worthylake, his wife Ann and daughter Ruth were returning to the island when a sudden gale overturned their rowboat. Tragically, all three drowned and they are buried together under a single stone in the Copp's Hill Burying Ground in Boston. Ironically, the second keeper assigned to the station, Robert Saunders, drowned within a few days of his appointment. John Hayes took over as the third keeper on November 18, 1718 and served the light station well, retiring on August 22, 1733. During his fifteen year tenure, he survived several storms and participated in several rescues of shipwreck survivors.

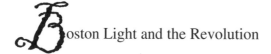oston Light and the Revolution

On December 16, 1773 a group of angry Boston citizens threw tea into Boston Harbor to protest the British taxation of the colony. The Boston Tea Party, as it was called, resulted in the British Parliament passing the Boston Port Act in March 1774, closing the port of Boston to all commercial traffic until the colony paid for the tea. On May 13, General Thomas Gage arrived in Boston to enforce the Port Act. He took command of four regiments of British Red Coats that arrived shortly thereafter and by June, Boston Harbor was closed. Over six hundred ships would be denied access to the harbor, and Gage and his British troops were very unpopular.

As part of their enforcement strategy, the British took control of Boston Light and the colonists then made two attempts to destroy it. The first attempt was led by Major Vose on July 20, 1775. With a small group of Continental soldiers, he rowed out to the island and burned every part of the structure that was wood. The Americans returned safely home but by the end of July, the British forces had rebuilt the light station. Major Tupper then attacked and destroyed the lighthouse but during this encounter, several of the English troops stationed on the island and one of the American soldiers were killed.

By March 17, 1776, the Dorchester Heights section outside of Boston had been fortified by General Washington. Knowing the futility of attacking the stronghold, British General William Howe withdrew his army from Boston and sailed to Nova Scotia. The British Navy finally withdrew on June 13, 1776 but before they left, the British Commander set a time bomb at the lighthouse as a message for the Boston Patriots. The charge did its job and the light was destroyed.

A new seventy-five-foot rubble stone tower was erected in 1783 and six years later, it was turned over to the Federal government. From 1783 to 1811, twenty-eight years, Thomas Knox served as the keeper of Boston Light. Since that time, the light has only been extinguished during the period of World War II from 1941 until July 2, 1945. Today, the flashing signal from Boston Light continues to guide ships safely into the harbor. America's first lighthouse is also its last - it is the only lighthouse still manned by Coast Guard keepers.

*T*he Revolution and Portsmouth Light

*D*ifferent from the other New England states, New Hampshire's coastline is only eighteen miles long and Portsmouth Harbor Light is the only mainland lighthouse built on its shore. Over the years the light has had many different names. The original name, Fort William and Mary, was changed to Fort Constitution at the end of the Revolution. It has also been known as Fort Point, New Castle, and Portsmouth Harbor Light. The Portsmouth area is rich with maritime history. John Paul Jones lived in Portsmouth in 1777 while awaiting the completion of his ship the *Ranger*. The harbor is also the home of the Portsmouth Naval Shipyard, established June 12, 1800, which has played a vital role in the defense and security of the United States, particularly in the development and construction of submarines.

The first light to mark the harbor was installed in 1771. It consisted of nothing more than a lamp on a pole at Fort William and Mary, located about one mile in from the mouth of the Piscataqua River, one of the fastest running rivers on the continent. The soldiers stationed in this fortified area hoisted the lantern up the pole at sunset each day and lowered it at sunrise. A small tax was levied on local ship owners to pay for the minimal cost of maintaining the beacon.

Portsmouth Harbor Light   *U.S. Coast Guard Photo*

The Revolution gained momentum in the colonies after the British Parliament passed the Massachusetts Government Act in the spring of 1774 which nullified the charter. Virginia's Governor Dunmore dissolved the Virginia House of Burgesses on May 20. In October, the Massachusetts assembly met in Salem and reorganized as a provincial congress. Adjourning to Concord, they elected John Hancock president and formed a military organization of minutemen. Feelings were running high against the British and in December of 1774, the first overt act of the Revolution occurred at Fort William and Mary.

In order to arm the minutemen, supplies such as cannons, gunpowder and muskets had to be located, confiscated and hidden from the British. Paul Revere of Boston found out that the small fort in Portsmouth was stocked with supplies and weapons, and that the British were planning to garrison more soldiers there within a few days. He saddled up his horse and made a fast two day ride to Portsmouth where he met with the local seamen and patriots. They organized into a makeshift militia group and devised a plan to attack the fort. The old tavern was buzzing with excitement about the upcoming event and after several grogs, the men were ready. Armed with poles, pitchforks, a few guns and plenty of enthusiasm, they marched over to the fort.

The British Lieutenant in charge of the fort knew the odds were against him. He tried to reason with the noisy gang but to no avail. After a few tense moments, the two sides reached an agreement: the Portsmouth men would charge the fort and the British would fire over their heads as a gesture of defense before surrendering. The colonists captured the guns and supplies and the British troops left for Boston, unscathed. The supplies were transported and hidden in the Exeter/Newmarket area and some were eventually used against the British at the battle of Bunker Hill six months later.

When the war was over the name William and Mary disappeared rapidly and the Fort was renamed Fort Constitution. In 1784 Captain Titus Salter became the keeper at this historic site and he oversaw the building of a permanent wooden lighthouse tower. Five years later, President Washington visited

Portsmouth for four days and while fishing in a small wooden boat, he was knocked off his feet when a large breaker spun his craft around. Washington reportedly sported a large bruise for several days after his visit to the lighthouse. The present light, a forty-eight foot cast iron tower, was erected in 1877.

Thatchers Island Light and the Revolution

Just off the coast of Rockport, Massachusetts on Cape Ann, sits a barren fifty acre pile of ledge known as Thatchers Island. One of the first recorded shipwrecks on the island occurred in 1635 when the *Watch and Wait* smashed against the rocks in a storm. Anthony Thatcher and his wife were the only survivors in the tragic event which took the lives of twenty-one others. They were on their way from Ipswich to Marblehead when the storm hit. Reverend Avery, Thatcher's cousin, and his family were also on board. Avery was on his way to Marblehead to become the small seaport town's new preacher. The island was given to the Thachers to compensate them for their tragic loss.

After numerous other disasters, the Massachusetts Bay Colony authorized the construction of two granite light towers on the island in 1771. This was the fourth lighthouse erected north of Cape Cod to guide ships into the Boston area. Boston, Plymouth and Portsmouth were the other three stations. A Keeper Kirkwood was in charge of the light during the Revolution but he was removed because of his Tory connections and the lights in the two towers were extinguished for the duration of the war. The government authorized seven other dual towers which were built between 1768 and 1839: Matinicus Rock (ME), Newburyport (MA), Cape Elizabeth (ME), Bakers Island (MA), Plymouth (MA), Chatham (MA), and Highlands (NJ). Over a long period of time these lighthouses have been converted to one beacon.

During the Battle at Bunker Hill on June 17, 1775 the British suffered tremendous losses - over 1100 of their soldiers were killed. Captain Linzee of the British sloop-of-war the *Falcon* had supported his troops throughout the battle with sea fire and he was extremely frustrated over the outcome. In August 1775 he

50

decided to sail up to Thatchers Island and harass some of the patriots who were actively involved in the American cause for liberty. As he sailed around the island, he noticed some sheep grazing in a pasture just off Coffin's Beach on the southeastern side of the cape. Knowing the sheep would make a great meal for his hungry sailors, he ordered two barges with about fifty sailors to go in and bring back several animals.

Peter Coffin, a local farmer, was watching the ship carefully. As soon as he saw the sailors preparing the landing boats, he notified six other locals to hurry down to the shore, hide in the dunes and be prepared to fire their muskets. As the British boats came closer to the shore, the men beat on pails, shouted commands, and fired their muskets across the beach. A stray ball hit the sword of a British Lieutenant standing in the front end of the barge. Convinced that a good sized regiment awaited him, he returned to the *Falcon* without the mutton.

Linzee then sighted a ship coming around Thachers light. He could not ignore the opportunity to capture some valuable commodities, and he immediately gave chase. After a quick pursuit, the ship yielded, but when they boarded her, the British discovered the cargo consisted of nothing but sand. An angry Captain Linzee sailed back to Thatchers Island and cruised back and forth in front of the granite ledge.

In the next three days he captured one small schooner and watched another escape into Gloucester Harbor. The small craft grounded on a sandbar and Linzee sent in a barge to board the ship. He watched in astonishment as a small mob of Gloucester fishermen fired upon his men. Several British sailors on the barge were hit. Linzee could no longer control his rage and he positioned the *Falcon* so its cannons could fire broadsides at the town. He ordered the cannons to fire and shouted his command, "Burn the darn town down."

Since cannon fire is not precisely accurate, the gunners aimed their shots at the church steeple, the central point of the town. Any misses would surely hit a building or house near the church. Unfortunately for Captain Linzee, the only thing they hit was a hog owned by one of the church deacons. A few of the men in the barge managed to scramble back to the ship but the British sailors on shore were taken prisoner. Linzee had met his match, ordered the sails hoisted and sailed away from Thatchers Island for the last time.

When the Gloucester fishermen gathered together after the incident, they discovered one man was missing from their ranks. The only thing he left behind was his hat. Since it appeared that Linzee had not captured any prisoners, to this day no one knows for certain what happened to that lone fisherman. Scandalous rumors circulated throughout the town that he had simply run away. As the father of thirteen children, he had been known to complain of confusion in his household and many folks figured that he had seized the opportunity to leave his responsibilities behind. Others considered him a dedicated colonial hero who was captured or drowned and washed out to sea.

Lighthouses during the War of 1812

Chesapeake and Shannon

Just off the shore from Boston Head Light a famous naval battle took place on June 1, 1813. The HMS *Shannon*, a fifty-two gun frigate under Captain Broke, challenged the forty-one gun frigate *Chesapeake*, commanded by Captain James Lawrence. The *Chesapeake's* crew was new and had not yet been tested in battle. The *Shannon* however, had been one of the ships blockading Boston Harbor and Broke's crew was seasoned.

A short time after rounding the point of Boston Head Light, the *Chesapeake* met the *Shannon*. Within fifteen minutes of making contact, she was boarded by the British as Broke's more experienced gunnery crew had smashed the gunwales of the *Chesapeake* in the first broadside. After taking two hits, one in the leg and another through his body, Captain Lawrence was taken below decks. Barely audible, he cried out, "Don't give up the ship. Fight on until they strike or sink."

In the fifteen minute bloody exchange, Broke lost a fourth of his crew and Lawrence one-third of his. Broke was also wounded. The British boarding party was successful and the *Chesapeake* struck her colors. Again, Lawrence cried out, "Keep the guns going. Don't give up the ship." It was too late, the battle was over, and the British took the *Chesapeake* to Halifax, Nova Scotia. Lawrence and twenty-one year old Lieutenant Ludlow, died at sea just before the ship arrived in Halifax and both officers were buried on foreign soil.

When news of these events reached Salem, the local seamen demanded that the bodies of the two American officers be returned for proper burial on their own soil. On July 20, 1813 the Rev. Dr. Bentley notified President Madison that Captain George Crowinshield Jr. would sail up to Halifax under a flag of truce and bring them back, at no cost to the U.S. Government. Permission was granted and the British agreed to cooperate. The brig *Henry*, with a crew of volunteers, arrived in Halifax on August 7, 1813 and retrieved the remains. When the ship returned and sailed past the two lights at Bakers Island on August 18, the crew noticed the keeper's house had been draped in black as a tribute to the fallen heroes.

The following Monday a funeral service was held in Salem. Boats filled the harbor, many exhibiting "Free Trade and Sailors Rights" signs. The bodies of the two men were rowed into Phillips Wharf where they were received by two hearses. A long parade formed as six captains and two lieutenants from the U.S. Navy walked slowly and silently as pallbearers next to their dead comrades. The scene was solemn and quiet as the procession made its way to the church. Flags were at half mast; business in the town had been suspended for the day; buildings were draped in black; bells tolled every few minutes. Spectators crowded the parade route. The Salem Artillery fired a gun salute from a distance away. The church overflowed as Judge Story gave the eulogy. The remains of these two heroes were taken to the Crowninshield tomb to await passage to New York for final burial. "Don't give up the ship!" later became the rallying cry for the U.S. Navy.

Casco Bay, Maine

Another interesting battle in the War of 1812 occurred in Casco Bay, just off of the Portland, Maine shore. On September 5, 1813 Captain Samuel Blythe of the British ship HMS *Boxer* was sailing down from the Monhegan area when Lieutenant Commandant William Burrows, of the American brig *Enterprise*, sailed out of Portland Harbor to challenge him. The two ships met about four miles south of Pemaquid and engaged in a battle which only lasted a few minutes before both commanders were instantly killed. The Americans were victorious and brought the captured British ship into Portland. The two Captains' bodies were brought to shore and they were buried side-by-side in the old graveyard on Munjoy Hill, overlooking Portland Harbor. Lieutenant Burrows was twenty-eight years old and Captain Blythe was twenty-nine.

Scituate Light

A twenty-five foot stone tower, thirty feet above sea level, and a keepers house were built in 1811 to mark the entrance to Scituate Harbor in Massachusetts. The first keeper commissioned to the light was Simeon Bates, who occupied the light station with his wife and nine children. Two of his daughters, Rebecca and Abigail, were teenagers. The heroic actions of these two young girls on a cool crisp September day in 1814 saved the families of Scituate from instant disaster.

On June 18, 1812 a Declaration of War against England was approved by President Madison after it passed the United States House of Representatives and the Senate (79-49 and 19-13). This war was not popular with many Americans. British frigates sailed up and down the New England Coast and harassed the small seaports, relentlessly pursuing the fishermen and small coastal schooners that worked out of the harbors. The British maintained an effective blockade and the local maritime commerce suffered. This caused despair for the residents, since seaport towns depended upon the freedom of movement on the sea for a living. The townspeople were also in constant fear of undergoing a shelling from the British warships. Scituate villagers experienced these same hardships and fears.

On that September morning in 1814, Keeper Bates and his wife Rachel had taken six of their children to town with them to do some errands. Rebecca and Abigail stayed behind to watch over their younger brother and to take care of the station. They climbed the tower to trim the wick and clean the glass in the lantern room. From their high vantage point the girls saw a large British man-of-war come to in the deep waters off the southern point. Looking through the telescope they could make out the name *La Hogue.*

Scituate Light   *U.S. Coast Guard Photo*

The British were loading five longboats with Red Coats preparing to ransack the tiny town. The girls knew that British soldiers had landed in other small harbors and looted and vandalized the villages, leaving behind broken homes and businesses. Because of this constant threat during the War of 1812, many seaport town residents stored their valuables and family heirlooms in hidden caves or outbuildings outside of their towns. Local "security guards" were hired to watch over the hidden goods. This not only protected them from a British invasion but also from local thieves.

Rebecca and Abigail Bates were well aware of the pending disaster and they sprang into action. They first sent their little brother scampering into town with the news to warn the locals. Then they took a fife and drum and hid in the rocks. They started to play muster music as loud as they could. Rebecca's hands were blistering with the forced energy of her drumming and Abigail was almost out of breath as she blew fiercely into the high pitched flute. The British heard the commotion and thought a large contingent of Colonial forces were organizing to repel them. The captain of *La Hogue* also heard the music and battle call. Not knowing what to expect, he sent up a signal flag calling the troops in the boats back to the ship. The British fired one shot from a twenty pound cannon which missed the lighthouse and fell into the bay. The mighty warship with its invading Red Coats turned back to sea. Rebecca and Abigail had stopped the invasion and saved the town.

akers Island Light

About five miles out to sea from the harbor of Salem, Massachusetts, two lighted beacons were built on each end of a keeper's home on Bakers Island. They were first lit on January 3, 1798. In 1916 the tall tower known as "Mr. Lighthouse" was the sole light when the smaller "Mrs. Lighthouse" was removed.

During the War of 1812 the most famous warship of the American Navy, the USS *Constitution*, was almost sunk and destroyed just off Bakers Island. On December 18, 1814 the *Constitution* sailed out of Boston Harbor into a stormy sea with a light wind blowing. The thirty-six year old Captain, Charles Stewart, had a fine reputation for heroic service, having captured the schooner *Pictou* and three smaller vessels earlier that year. The British Navy, maintaining a tight blockade along the coast, had two of their large ships just a few miles offshore of Boston Harbor. The *Tenedos* and the *Endymion* were following Captain Stewart as he set sail for Salem. As they were closing in just one mile from the lights at Bakers Island, the *Constitution* hit a calm. Stewart had his crew toss every item overboard that could be considered dispensable.

The captain had to get "Old Ironsides" safely into Marblehead Harbor, past the rocky ledges and small islands and under the guns of Fort Sewall. At the time he did not know that

Bakers Island Light   *U.S. Coast Guard Photo*

USS Constitution by Photographer's Mate Chief John E. Gay   *U.S. Navy Photo*

the fort had only eight cannon balls to fire, and almost no powder. Captain Stewart had a gunners mate onboard named Nathaniel Green who had been raised in Marblehead as a fisherman. Green knew the entrance to the harbor - where the ledges were and where the deep water passage was situated. Captain Stewart made him his pilot. At the same time another expert on the harbor, Keeper Joseph Perkins, rowed out from Bakers Island to help the ship.

As the British frigates bore down, it appeared they might be able to catch the *Constitution* in a cross fire. A slight breeze finally came up and Green and Perkins maneuvered the ship on a delicate course, zigzagging past the perilous rocks to find the natural channel. In a short time the ship was safely behind the guns of Fort Sewall. The British Captains decided that the risks were too great to pass the fort and enter the difficult harbor and they sailed back towards Boston.

In the meantime, the Marblehead Militia was arriving at the harbor area and a group of Salem men, led by Reverend

Bentley (in full preacher's gown), appeared hauling a cannon. The troops were ready. About two hundred Sea Fencibles gathered on the shore. Captain Joseph Ropes of Salem took command. These volunteers were too old to fight in active service but young enough to help defend the coast. At the next high tide the *Constitution* sailed into Salem Harbor which was considered a safer port. Captain Stewart sailed out of Salem within the next few days, grateful for the help from the Marblehead and Salem patriots.

Wives and Families of the Lights

Many stories have been told about the challenges faced by lighthouse keepers, but the stories of the keeper's families have often been overlooked. Wives were the keeper's partners and they did all of the duties required of their husbands but were never paid. They were also expert sailors, cooks, and jacks-of-all-trades. The Lighthouse Service, and later the Coast Guard, received the services of two workers for the price of one.

The women and the young families of the keepers had to know all of the equipment at the station and how to use it. First and foremost, they learned how to keep the beacon shining. Fueled by kerosene from 1846 until the early 1930's, the light itself was complicated; the mechanism running it was tiny and delicate. Silver plated reflectors rotated around the lantern, powered by clockwork motors with windup weights. The bell and fog horn systems had to be operational and properly maintained. Ropes and wires had to be spliced. Equipment needed constant painting and cleaning. The work had to be done, and if the keeper was ill or unable to get back to the island, his family was responsible for the lighthouse.

Waving good-bye to the keeper when he left the island for the mainland was a time of uncertainty for the family he left behind. They were never sure when, if ever, he would safely return. Heavy seas could suddenly surge and sink his row boat; a storm might arise without warning, and smash his craft against the rocks on shore. If he left the island and the weather turned while he was on the mainland, he might not be able to get back to the lighthouse for days. While the keepers were at shore, they were able to visit and talk with other people, but the family left behind was still alone. It could be months before they left the bleak station. Their only correspondence with others was by mail, and even that could be delayed for weeks at a time during bad weather. Isolation was a major problem.

In his book, "Lighthouses of the Maine Coast and The Men Who Keep Them," Robert Thayer Sterling describes the life of Mrs. Corbett, wife of Captain Corbett, keeper at Little River in Maine. They had a large family with eight children in school who had to be rowed over to the mainland every day. It was a short distance, but a miserable row in bad weather. Her father was also a keeper, and Mrs. Corbett related a story to Sterling about an evening during a winter storm when she and her mother heard a knock on the island station door. A sailor had left his vessel moored off the mainland and tried to row to shore, but the heavy surf diverted him to the island. A young girl at that time, Mrs. Corbett and her mother took the freezing man into the living quarters and nursed him back to health throughout the night. With little medical training, it was a difficult challenge, but they faced it and saved a life - the most rewarding duty a keeper and his family could perform.

Sterling writes of another episode which occurred on Mt. Desert Island, December 9, 1902. In the early morning, before sunrise, on an extremely cold day, the ocean tug *Astral* went aground. The sea spray and foam blowing in the gale force winds froze on the surface of the rocks, making for a difficult and slippery rescue. Seventeen men were brought to the keeper's quarters and the two wives on the island set up a makeshift hospital. They took care of frostbite; prepared hot lemonade; cooked meals; administered quinine pills and made the crew comfortable for several days. The men survived and despite the severity of their conditions, they were able to walk down to the rescue ship when it arrived. The women at the light station were ready to meet any situation at any time, and as some of them said, "No matter how bad things get, you have probably seen worse."

Mt. Desert Island Light   *U.S. Coast Guard Photo*

Mary Abbie Williams served with her husband William on Boon Island Light from 1885 until 1911 – a total of twenty-six years and sixteen days on a three acre ledge, six miles out to sea, in a house that was flooded out in every storm. On one of her trips to the mainland, she and William were caught in a dramatic change of weather and their small sailboat was overturned. She was swept under the sail, but was able to work her way out from under the water to the bow, and she held on with William until a rescue ship appeared on the scene. At her sister's house on the mainland, they changed their clothes and then went about their business as if nothing out of the ordinary had happened that day.

Edward Rowe Snow, the well known twentieth century lighthouse historian in his book "Famous Lighthouses of New England" (Oct. 1945) mentions several exceptional lighthouse women who had some rare experiences, among them were Abbie Burgess, Ida Lewis and Maria Bray.

Matinicus Rock Light   *U.S. Coast Guard Photo*

ℐbbie Burgess Grant and Matinicus Rock Light

"Sometimes I think the time is not far distant when I shall climb these lighthouse stairs no more. It has almost seemed to me that the light was a part of myself...Those old lamps – as they were when my father lived on Matinicus Rock – are so thoroughly impressed on my memory that even now I often dream of them... When I dream of them it always seems to me that I have been away a long while, and I am trying to get back in time to light the lamps...I wonder if the care of the lighthouse will follow my soul after it has left this worn-out body! If I ever have a gravestone, I would like it to be in the form of a lighthouse or beacon."

Abbie Burgess Grant – from a letter to a friend
from "The Century; a popular quarterly" June 1897

$\mathcal{I}$n 1827, two wooden towers were erected on Matinicus Rock, thirty acres of solid ledge located twenty-two miles out into the mighty Atlantic. In 1847 the wooden structures were replaced by two strong tall granite towers. Considered one of the most isolated posts in the entire lighthouse chain, this station has the distinction of being the farthest lighthouse out to sea off the coast of Maine. It was a lonely outpost for the families who tendered it. Prior to 1861 the government did not consider it necessary to have more than one keeper at a station because the keeper's wife and family were considered part of the workforce. This was the situation on Matinicus Rock.

Samuel Burgess was appointed as keeper of Matinicus in the spring of 1853. He sailed out to the desolate island with his chronically ill wife (a very feeble woman), his four girls, and a son who left the island a short time later as a member of a fishing boat crew. Abbie, at fourteen, was the oldest girl. She adapted to her new lifestyle rapidly, and in a short time was able to work in complete harmony with her father, maintaining the light and the station. Within a year her dad considered her the assistant keeper. He had full confidence in her ability to take over his duties if an emergency occurred.

When Abbie first came to the island she enjoyed reading the logbook written by the former keepers. Account after account told of giant waves crashing over the island and smashing against the keeper's house. During these storms, the only safe refuge on the island was in the damp confining towers, built from dovetailed granite blocks. Each stone weighed just over one ton and some were anchored with massive steel rods to the blocks above and below. Although the base of the tower measured twenty-five feet across, because of the thickness of the stone walls, the inside opening was only about eight feet in diameter. Circular steel stairs rose up from the base to the watch room. Some of the logs described storms that kept the keepers and their families in the tower watch rooms for days.

In January of 1856, with clear weather ahead for a few days, Captain Burgess decided to row over to Matinicus Island, a distance of about six miles. The weather was fine when he left, but took a turn for the worse the next day when he was scheduled to return to the rock. Abbie, her ailing mother and three young sisters were alone at the light station. As the weather worsened, she knew her father was stranded on the other island, and she started to prepare the lights for the storm. The sky turned dark gray, the wind howled and the sea began to rise.

Soon the waves were crashing over the rocks on the island and smashing against the keeper's quarters. Battling the wind and the slippery rocks, timing her trips between the ebb and flow of the rushing water, Abbie moved her mother and sisters into the safety of the tower. Then she decided to rescue the chickens she kept in a small outbuilding near the tower. By now the water was knee deep; the surf was smashing across the island. She waded into the icy brine and with great determination, she was able to rescue four of the five hens before a breaker knocked the coop into the sea.

During this ordeal, Abbie kept the lights burning in both towers. There were fourteen lamps and she had to keep them fueled, trim the wicks, and clean the reflectors and lens. She also had to take care of her mom and sisters in the watch room. It was a tremendous responsibility for a seventeen year old girl, but Abbie met the challenge. Although the storm subsided over the next few days, the sea between Matinicus Island and Matinicus Rock did not let up and it was four weeks before her father returned to his post. Throughout that period, Abbie kept the lights lit.

A year later, the cache of supplies on the island was running critically low and Captain Burgess was forced to leave the station for more food. He waited for a run of good weather and set off for Matinicus Island. Again, the weather turned and he could not get back. Abbie's brother was on the rock at this time, and knowing that his family faced possible starvation, he decided to sail the six miles for supplies. As the women watched his sail disappear into the rough surf they were acutely aware of the fact that once again, they were alone on the ledge in a severe storm. They did not know if their father or brother had ever reached the island safely. The good news finally came three weeks later when early one morning, Abbie sighted the sailboat on the horizon, heading back to Matinicus Rock. By the time her father and brother returned with food, she had limited the daily ration to one egg and a cup of corn mush each, and even that was almost gone. This time, she had kept the lights burning for twenty-one days. She was soon referred to as the "guiding spirit of the rock" by the passing mariners.

Samuel Burgess retired from the United States Lighthouse Service and left Matinicus Rock Light in 1861. Abbie, the seasoned assistant lighthouse keeper, stayed behind to help the new keepers, Captain John Grant and his family, become familiar with the duties and maintenance of the light. Captain Grant's son Isaac took a particular interest in the light, and in Abbie. They soon fell in love and married within a year. She was officially appointed the assistant keeper at Matinicus, and served on the rock with her husband until they were reassigned to White Head Light in 1875. They had four children before they left Matinicus Rock.

Captain John Grant remained head keeper at Matinicus

White Head Light   *U.S. Coast Guard Photo*

for twenty-nine years, retiring in 1890 at the age of eighty-five. His son William then became the head keeper. Abbie and her husband Isaac retired from White Head in May of 1890. She died in 1892 at the age of fifty-three years old. A small iron lighthouse marker stands next to her grave at the Spruce Head Cemetery just southeast of Rockland, Maine. It is a small tribute to a woman of great courage who gave so much of herself to make life secure and safe for others. Her outstanding deeds will always shine in the hearts of those who appreciate a life devoted to duty.

*M*aria Bray and Thachers Island Light

*I*n 1861, two granite towers were constructed on Thachers Island on Cape Ann off the coast of Rockport, Massachusetts. The one hundred and twenty-four foot towers replaced existing structures and were built to accommodate new first order Fresnal lenses. In 1864, Captain Alexander Bray, a disabled Civil War veteran, secured the appointment of keeper at the lighthouse. He and his wife Maria moved to the island and took up residence in the two story keeper's home. They adapted to their island lifestyle and their new duties and responsibilities as the keepers of the Twin Lights.

A few days before Christmas, the assistant keeper on the island developed a high fever and Captain Bray decided to take him over to the mainland for medical attention. Bray left at sunrise and his wife Maria stayed behind to run the island. Neither she nor her husband sensed what was in store. Before noon a heavy snowstorm developed and strong winds whipped up the sea. Maria realized that her husband would not be able to get back to the island. Alone with just her infant son Tom and her fourteen year old nephew, Sidney Haskell, Maria was responsible for keeping the two lights burning. The lights could not go out under any circumstances, especially in the severe weather.

Her first reaction was to get the little boy in warm clothes. She bundled him up in jackets, pants and blankets. Her next thought was to get Sydney and the baby over to one of the towers;

the north tower seemed further away from the direct onslaught of the whirling snow. Maria fought her way through the blinding blizzard with a child under her arm and fourteen year old Sydney holding her hand. Blinded by the stinging hail, blowing snow and ice, she leaned forward against the force of the wind to gain some stability and footing on the slippery ground. She could hear the pounding surf a few feet away and prayed she would reach the tower before a mighty wave washed them out to sea. The storm was attacking the island with a tremendous fury. Finally they reached the tower and with Sydney's help, she pulled the heavy door open.

Inside, she climbed the one hundred and forty-eight steps to the watch room, where she lit a small heater to provide warmth for the baby. She then ignited the wick in the light and set the oil lever which would control the burning of the flame. Next, she climbed down to the base of the tower, plunged back into the storm, and was able to make her way to the bell house to wind up the bell. The snow was drifting deeper and deeper but she realized she must get over to the south tower and light that lantern. She repeated this journey - down one tower, across the island through the snow and storm to the other tower, up the second tower – almost every five hours, for three days, until the weather finally broke on Christmas Eve day.

At the first sign of the storm letting up, Keeper Bray left the mainland. Using the Twin Light beacons as a guide, he was able to fight the still heavy seas and reach the island by that afternoon. The Bray's had a cheerful reunion, and probably their most memorable and thankful Christmas Day. Maria Bray, like many keeper's wives, demonstrated a spirit of courage and daring that would not be denied.

Ida Lewis and Lime Rock Light

Ida Lewis was born February 25, 1842 in Newport, RI. In 1854 her father, Hosea Lewis, was transferred from duty on a revenue cutter to the lighthouse service because of failing health.

Ida Lewis Light (Lime Rock Light)   *U.S. Coast Guard Photo*

He was assigned to Lime Rock Light, an island one third of a mile from the Newport mainland. Ida had three younger siblings, two brothers and a sister, and it soon became her responsibility to row them back and forth to the mainland each day so they could attend the local school. She became proficient at rowing, and developed great strength.

Four years after his appointment, Keeper Lewis suffered a stroke. He recovered, but was unable to perform the tasks necessary to maintain the light. Ida, at sixteen, helped her mother with all of the lighthouse duties. She thrived on the responsibility. She truly had salt in her veins. She could row a boat as well as any keeper, and was a powerful swimmer.

Within a year of assuming her father's duties, she made her first rescue. The waters off Newport were heavily sailed and if the turbulent tides and unrelenting sea did not cause ships trouble, the stupidity of some of the sailors just might. On this particular day, one of four young men sailing by the island thought it would be fun to climb up the mast and rock the boat. It sure was fun as the boat turned upside down and all four men ended up in the sea. Ida launched her boat from Lime Rock and quickly rowed to their aid. The young men were frantic. Afraid of drowning, they tried to clutch onto Ida's row boat. With her raw strength and common sense, she maneuvered the skiff into several positions and pulled each of them into the boat, one at a time.

A short time later, three drunken soldiers crossing the harbor kicked a hole in the side of their boat and it started to sink. Two of them made it to shore on their own, but Ida had to row out and retrieve the third. It was reported that the man was so heavy she could not lift him into the boat. She tied a rope around him and towed him to shore.

In 1867, three men herding a sheep along the Newport wharf were surprised when the animal suddenly ran off the end of the pier and landed in the water. They grabbed the nearest boat and set off to rescue the animal, but were soon capsized by heavy seas. Ida launched her lifeboat and went to their rescue. She pulled the men in, deposited them on shore, and then went back to sea and brought in the sheep. This was one of her favorite rescues and she would often tell of it when she took the time to reminisce. A year later she rescued a thief who stole a boat to make an escape. He grounded the boat late at night and Ida did not discover him until morning. By the time she rescued him, as she said, "He was shaking and God-blessing me, and praying to be set on shore."

In 1869, two soldiers returning to Fort Adams hitched a ride on a sailboat piloted by a young boy. The lad mistakenly turned the boat into a strong wind and it overturned. The three struggled to hang onto the boat as Ida and her brother Hosea rowed to their rescue. Just as the boy went under, Ida grabbed him and pulled him into the rescue boat. She and Hosea then rescued the two soldiers.

In 1879, Ida was officially named the keeper at Lime Rock. On February 4, 1881 two more soldiers were rescued by Ida Lewis. They were attempting to cross the frozen harbor on foot, when the ice gave way and they went under. Ida heard their cries for help, and without regard for her own safety, grabbed a rope and ran across the ice and pulled both men up out of the hole. She was awarded the Gold Life-Saving Medal for this rescue on July 16, 1881.

She was credited with saving at least eighteen lives, but probably saved more. She gained national notoriety and was the subject of many articles in newspapers and journals. She was visited by many members of the upper-class Newport society including the Astors and Vanderbilts. President Ulysses S. Grant scheduled a visit with her when he was in Newport.

Ida passed away while on duty at Lime Rock Light on October 24, 1911 and she is buried in the Newport Cemetery. She was sixty-nine years old. For fifty-seven years she performed her duty, faithfully giving of herself to her fellow man. After the state of Rhode Island changed the name of Lime Rock to Ida Lewis Rock, the Coast Guard renamed the lighthouse Ida Lewis Lighthouse in her honor. No other lighthouse is named for a keeper. As another special honor, on April 12, 1997 a new Keeper Class Buoy Tender was launched by the Coast Guard; the lead ship is the *Ida Lewis* (WLM 551). Two other ships in this class are the *Abbie Burgess* (WLM 553) and the *Maria Bray* (WLM 562).

WLM Ida Lewis Launching   *U.S. Coast Guard Photo*

Connie Scovill Small

Connie Small was born June 4, 1901. Her grandfather was a sea captain, her uncle was a shipmaster and light keeper, and her sister married a lighthouse keeper. While in charge of the Quoddy Head Life Saving Station, her father was credited with saving the lives of many shipwrecked sailors. As a child Connie accompanied her father on rescue missions, carrying the cannon powder used to shoot the breeches buoy to stranded mariners. As a young woman, she married Elson Small, a merchant seaman during World War I, who would become a lighthouse keeper for the next twenty-eight years, with Connie standing by his side.

From 1920 to 1939 Connie and Elson were under the jurisdiction of the United States Lighthouse Service. From 1939 until 1948 they were part of the Coast Guard. Connie has been called "the first lady of the light" and President Bush Sr. referred to her as his "eleventh point of light". She is nationally known and has appeared on most major television networks at some time or another. People are drawn to her because of her remarkable life. She has lived what most people only write and read about. Her life has been devoted to others, but filled with loneliness, as she served on desolate, almost abandoned light stations. She fought the sea and braved the elements while keeping the light and signal working so ships and crews could pass safely by her shore.

She has shown great strength, courage and endurance with every inch of her five-foot frame and every ounce of her ninety-eight pounds. She never let down, no matter how great the obstacles or tough the job. She took pride in her work and her spirit never ended. Her lighthouse experiences are filled with remarkable deeds which she has written about in her best selling book "The Lighthouse Keeper's Wife." Connie's love of life and dedication to others never ends. When she turned ninety-six she had given over five hundred and twenty-one lectures to schools, civic groups and colleges. At age 100, Connie now has a total of over five hundred and fifty lectures, including one to Case Medical College.

Connie is a living legend. Her lighthouse experience taught her to always look up and never look down. When she climbed the outside tower of one of her first lighthouses she did not think she could do it - thirty-four slippery rungs on the outside of a tower, straight up to a square hole through which she would have to climb to get to a steel platform, followed by another eight rungs up to a steel door. One slip and the swirling tide would carry her directly out to sea with no chance for survival. Imagine trying to grab the first few rungs while popping up and down in a small peapod boat. Just standing up in the boat provided a chance of

Connie Scovill Small

being knocked overboard. Well, Connie figured out fast that she better not look down. "You can do it!" shouted Elson. "Don't ever look down." She did it and her first lighthouse lesson would stay with her the rest of her life.

Connie also has another great lighthouse philosophy and that is that people operate from the inside out. Just like the beacons she tendered, which shine from the inside, she has lived and thought with her heart. Her loving actions come from within her heart. Connie has built her life around the premise of love, compassion and care. The spirit of the lighthouse is one of brotherhood and sisterhood. We are all peers, we are all equal, and we connect as we try and make your journey as safe and seaworthy as possible.

Connie is the spirit of the lighted beacons she so nobly tendered. She shines from within and from without, illuminating a life filled with care and love. As a lighthouse keeper's wife, a dean of a college, an author and a sought after lecturer, she is the symbol of trust, hope and security. Connie Small is truly the "first lady of the light" and a legacy of her time.

The above talk was given by the author at Connie's 100th birthday party which was sponsored by the American Lighthouse Foundation and the United States Coast Guard.

West Quoddy Light

Located on the easternmost point of land in the continental United States, the red stripes make it more visible for passing ships to see during a snow squall. Built in 1807 it was rebuilt in 1858. In the early 1900's this station was given a five tube radio set by Mr. Atwater Kent, who summered on the coast of Maine.

West Quoddy Light   *U.S. Coast Guard Photo*

Petit Manan Light

The second tallest lighthouse in Maine, its granite tower was built in 1855 and stands one hundred and nineteen feet high. The first tower was built in 1817. It sits on a small island two and a half miles out to sea from the headland of Petit Manan Point. The nearest town is Milbridge. It once held the record for the most consecutive days the foghorn blew steadily. In 1869 a steam fog horn was installed, which operated from rainwater collected in roof gutters on the keeper's dwelling that was piped over to the engine propelling the horn.

In the winter months, because of ice buildup around the boat slip, keepers have spent as many as five weeks in isolation because boats could not depart or arrive. When telephone cables were installed, storms would sweep them away, which added to the total seclusion.

Petit Manan Light   *U.S. Coast Guard Photo*

*B*ass Harbor Head Light

*L*ocated on the southwest point of Mt. Desert this is one of the most photographed lighthouses in Maine. It was built in 1858 on one of the most picturesque ledges on the Maine Coast. At first glance, the brick cylindrical tower connected to the keeper's house looks as though it would be impossible to build on such a location, but here it stands.

Bass Harbor Light   *U.S. Coast Guard Photo*

*O*wls Head

*O*wls Head was built in 1825 on a high wave-swept promontory south of Rockland Harbor. The tower, separated from the keeper's house by a long stairway, is only twenty feet tall but it sits a hundred feet above the high water line. Surrounded by spruce trees this location is rich in scenery. It was first illuminated in September of 1825. In September of 1842 the American steam frigate *Missouri* sailed by the lighthouse to the delight of hundreds of people who had lined up to watch her enter Rockland Harbor.

Owls Head Light   *U.S. Coast Guard Photo*

Many shipwrecks have been recorded on the shores around the headlands. Edward Rowe Snow in his book "Famous Lighthouses of New England" has recorded one of the most dramatic and bizarre stories ever to be told. He writes of a coastal schooner caught in the storm of December 22, 1850, one of five vessels thrown ashore in subzero weather by the thunderous sea. The ships were grounded between Owls Head and Spruce Head. Three people were aboard the schooner, the mate, his bride-to-be, and a deck hand. Caught on a ledge, the boat hung up high and dry, but large waves tossed freezing spray against it and the ship started to be encased by ice.

The mate, realizing they would all freeze to death, had the girl lie down next to a rail and he wrapped her up with a heavy wool blanket. He laid down next to her, covered himself with another part of the blanket, and then instructed the deckhand to lay down next to him and cover himself with the remaining end of the blanket. Though under cover, the pounding surf and spray soon froze over their bodies and the three were enclosed by ice so thick that the mate and his future bride could not breathe. The deckhand kept chopping with his knife to leave a tiny opening through which he could get air.

When dawn broke the deckhand was able to break free, but it appeared the other two had suffocated. He climbed over the side of the ship, made his way through the glacial water, and headed up to the light station to seek help. The frigid air was piercing his lungs but he managed to alert Keeper Masters at the light station. He blurted out his story and fainted. Masters organized a rescue party and they quickly located the schooner. They boarded her and found the young girl and mate encased in ice. They chipped away the ice and brought the frozen bodies up to a nearby home. Using partially frozen water and raising the temperature slowly, they began a deliberate, tedious thawing process. Working the hands and feet and massaging the bodies, the rescue crew saw the two corpses begin to waken from what Mr. Snow called "their deathlike sleep." This seemed to be a miracle; after more than three hours of nursing, the young couple had been revived. After one and a half months of tender care the couple was able to leave, and the following June they were married.

Pemaquid Point Light

Built in 1827 and rebuilt in 1857, the light station tower is thirty feet tall and is located on top of a unique rock formation. This long ledge of rocks runs parallel with the ocean, extending out to sea for several hundred yards. The sea swept granite bluff creates a beautiful setting for a picture.

The ledges in and around Pemaquid have seen their share of shipwrecks. One of the first wrecks was the ship *Angel Gabriel* in 1635. John Cogswell and his family, one of the early settlers in the area, had just left the ship after arriving from England. The next day they watched their vessel be taken under by an onslaught of severe weather. The Cogswells later traveled south to Ipswich, Massachusetts.

Pemaquid Point Light   *U.S. Coast Guard Photo*

 am Island Light

On the eastern side of Boothbay Harbor sits Ram Island Light, built on an island in 1883. The name of this light is often confused with Ram Island Ledge Light which lies about a quarter of a mile offshore from Portland Head Light.

Ram Island Light was one of the last light stations to be built in Maine. The ocean in the geological area is interspersed with many small islands which were causing problems for the captains of the numerous ships sailing in and out of Boothbay Harbor. Before 1883 the wrecks were so frequent that local fishermen took it upon themselves to show some type of a signal. They lit lanterns in boxes and at one time, hung a lantern from a pole attached to a dory anchored off the point. The fishermen stopped on their way home from fishing to light the beacons.

There have been many stories associated with this island about some ghostly spirits that have kept the light shining. A lady in white holds a torch; an old fisherman lights a warning fire; whistles and horns blow during fogs when there were no horns or whistles on the island; these are just a few of the apparitions that haunt the island but protect the sailors.

When the lighthouse was built in 1883 and occupied by keepers, Mr. Robert Thayer Sterling in his book "Lighthouses of the Maine Coast and the Men Who Keep Them" (1935) reported that one of the first keepers had fifteen children born on the island. The next keeper had almost as many. There were certainly many hands to help with the chores. Growing up on a lighthouse was a great experience and the children raised there were prepared to deal with life's challenges.

Ram Island Light   *U.S. Coast Guard Photo*

Matinicus Rock Light

Abbie Burgess left this small island ledge in 1875, having lived at the lighthouse for twenty-two of her thirty-six years. Her father-in-law remained as keeper until he retired in 1890 at the age of eighty-five. Her brother-in-law, Assistant Keeper William

80

Grant, who later succeeded his father as keeper, had two young sons on Matinicus who were well known up and down the coast for having constructed a miniature fishing village around a small rock pond on the island. They built a variety of boats, wharves, fish houses, nets and barrels in perfectly scaled detail. Local fishermen used to stop at the island just to marvel at the work. Grant and his wife also had a baby girl on the island, who died shortly after birth. They buried her in a rock crevice, closing the opening with bricks to protect her cherished remains from the sea.

Seguin Island Light

The second oldest lighthouse in Maine, Seguin Island, was built in 1795. It was rebuilt in 1820 and again in 1857. This light is the highest above sea level in the state of Maine. Its tower only stands fifty-three feet high but because it is on the highest point of the island, it is one hundred and eighty-six feet above the ocean. The beacon can be seen up to forty miles away.

Seguin Island Light   *U.S. Coast Guard Photo*

Seguin is located about two miles out to sea from Popham Beach. This station boasts one of the most powerful fog horns in the state. A blast of the horn during the frequent heavy fogs has been known to knock sea gulls out of the sky. The fog horn blows about ninety-five days a year. The first lighthouse was built under an order from President George Washington. Its first keeper was a veteran of the American Revolution, Major John Polereczky, who earned a salary of about three dollars and eighty-four cents a week.

Portland Head Light

Portland Head Light   *U.S. Coast Guard Photo*

Since 1791 this light station has been active. President George Washington signed the commission of Captain Joseph Greenleaf, the light's first keeper. Portland, Maine is the state's busiest harbor and Portland Head Light, located in the town of Cape Elizabeth, is Maine's oldest lighthouse. The tower is built of rubble stone taken from the local fields. Portland Head Light is one of the most visited and photographed light stations on the Atlantic coast.

During World War II from 1941-1945, a portion of the North Atlantic fleet was stationed here. War active ships of all sizes steamed in and out of these waterways twenty-four hours a day. Thirty thousand shipbuilders, men and women, built Liberty ships in the shipyards around Portland Harbor. They could complete one of these large cargo vessels in just fifty-two and a half days. Some of these ships were over four hundred feet long and had fifty-seven foot beams. As the Liberty ships sailed out for duty past the patriarch of Maine's lighthouses, Portland people knew the ships were strong and sturdy just like their lighthouse.

Henry Wadsworth Longfellow often visited Portland Head Light and later wrote in his lighthouse poem:

"Sail on; Sail on ye stately ships;
And with your floating bridge
the ocean span;
Be mine to guard this light
from all eclipse
Be yours to bring man near
unto man."

White letters painted on a rock mark the spot where the ship Annie C. Maguire went aground on the ledge a few yards off the south side of the lighthouse. On Christmas Eve, 1886 during a blinding blizzard, the captain of the ship tried to seek shelter in Portland Harbor. She had sailed up from Buenos Aires and was making her way to Quebec. Captain Thomas O'Neil lost his bearings and piled her high and dry on the rocky ledge. Keeper Joshua Strout did all within his power to warn the captain but it was to no avail. His son Joseph rigged up the boatswain chair and the captain, his wife and young son, and all fifteen crew members were rescued. Joshua Stout served as keeper from 1869-1904 and his son Joseph W. Strout served from 1904-1928. These two men with their families served for fifty-nine continuous uninterrupted years at Portland Head Light.

Ram Island Ledge Light

*R*am Island Ledge Light sits at the northern entrance to Portland Harbor. Because shipwrecks were common in this area, an iron spindle was erected on the ledge in 1855. This was replaced by a fifty foot wooden tripod in 1873 and finally, in 1905, a permanent granite tower was completed and lit. The keeper's living quarters were inside the tower. Three men, working a shift of two weeks on and one week off, manned the station until the light was automated in 1959.

Ram Island Ledge was deceiving since a large expanse of water covered part of the ledge at high tides. The submerged rocks tore up the hulls of many ships. These ledges were the site of fifteen major wrecks from 1866-1900. Because rescues were

Ram Island Ledge   *U.S. Coast Guard Photo*

84

speedy, few lives were lost, but thousands of dollars of cargo had been claimed by the sea. When the four hundred foot British steamship *California* and its crew of ninety-six grounded on the ledge in 1900, the Government decided that it was time to build a major lighthouse.

 oon Island

At one hundred and thirty-seven feet, this is the tallest standing lighthouse in New England. The present day granite tower was completed in 1855. The first structure was built in 1799 and the first manned lighthouse was built in 1811. When the Coast Guard took over the US Lighthouse Service in 1939, keepers assigned to Boon Island felt quarantined or punished, but in the last part of the nineteenth century, keepers appointed by the Lighthouse Service thrived there.

The remote location and harsh weather conditions were the main challenges faced by the keepers who kept their "solitary vigils" on this light. Boon Island Light is located over six miles out to sea off the coast of York and Kittery, Maine. The island is solid ledge seven hundred feet long by three hundred feet wide. There is no vegetation and the highest point of rock above sea level is only fourteen feet. There was not a lot of leg room and if a keeper did not see eye-to-eye with his mate, they could suffer through some long days and nights.

In the 1700's, before the first marker was erected, Boon was the site of several shipwrecks. The most famous was the wreck of the *Nottingham Galley* in 1710, during which the crew resorted to cannibalism in order to survive. After this incident, local fishermen lashed barrels of food to the highest rocks so any stranded mariners could survive on the stored food. This was a boon, or blessing, and grateful sailors named the island Boon.

Life as a keeper on Boon Island was dangerous and isolated, yet filled with intrigue. The following are some comments made by keepers who served there:

"When the feeling of closure sets in you have to get in the skiff and just row away from the island for a few hours."

"We had our own lobster traps set and we ate lobster three times a day. We traded lobsters for bread and milk with the local fishermen."

"All fresh water was rainwater. It was collected from the roofs of the buildings and stored in outside tanks. Any keeper who went to shore always carried back several five-gallon containers of water for a backup supply."

Boon Island

"The island was loaded with bats which made their home in the outbuildings. A lot of different species of birds migrate to the island as they move from one place to another."

"Birds fly into the glass protecting the light which caused a great mess and created a constant cleaning problem."

"Many seals and whales could be seen just off the island. The rocks are a favorite spot for the seals to sun and lounge."

"In any serious storm the keepers and their families had to go into the tower for protection and safety. Every good sized storm flowed through the first floor area of the living quarters. Most storms carried about five feet of water through the house. Seaweed and sand created havoc and were always a terrible mess to clean up."

"The fog horn would run as long as a week at a time. It was so loud, you could only talk to mates between blasts."

Most keepers' families lived on the mainland during the winter months and attended local schools. At one time, fifteen children lived on the island and a teacher was sent out to help.

Keepers have caught all sizes and types of fish out here. In 1914 the keeper caught an 898 lb. tuna which he sold to a local fish market for two cents a pound.

In the early 1900's a man from Boston arrived at the island, greased up his body and swam the 6.5 miles to the mainland. This was the first recorded swim from the island over to York, Maine.

It was not uncommon to watch an angry ocean carry away two or three of the full 2200-gallon tanks of oil and deposit them out to sea.

Some keepers were given duty time of three weeks on and one week off. Because of weather conditions, many could not get off the island on their free week.

Launching and landing a boat was tricky and had to be timed with the incoming surf. The boat had to slide down a skid with a rocky ledge on one side and large boulders on the other. Keepers were tossed into the ocean with their supplies when skiffs and peapods overturned or were smashed into the ledge. Timing was critical.

In 1960 the keepers noted a diesel leak in one of the tanks. A large amount of oil had run down into the boulders and was seeping into the sea. They called the commander and he told them to try and burn it off. After throwing some gas into the oil, they ignited the mess. The entire island was engulfed in a large black cloud. Apparently more oil had been lost than realized. Local Kittery and York residents immediately called the Coast Guard headquarters in Portsmouth to report a fire on Boon Island. The heat from the fire was so intense that water soaked rocks on the island started to explode, sending dangerous shrapnel in all directions, and the keepers had to lie on the floor of their stone house in order to escape the piercing rocks. All of the windows in the house were shattered. The officers and keepers were highly embarrassed but it was an interesting day on Boon Island.

Cape Neddick Light Station, Nubble Light

Driving into Maine, Nubble Light is the first lighthouse close to the mainland. Built on a nub of land at the end of a point known as Cape Neddick, it is one of the most photographed and painted lighthouses in America. The official Coast Guard name is the Cape Neddick Light Station but everyone, tourists and locals alike, refer to this beautiful lighthouse as "Nubble Light."

Built in 1879, the tower is forty-one feet high and eighty-eight feet above the high water mark. Thirteen feet in diameter, it is of brick construction covered by iron sheathing, with cement poured between the brick and the outer layer of the tower. The lens and light are enclosed in red Plexiglas. The light was automated in 1987.

The living quarters consist of a seven room house - three bedrooms, kitchen, dining room, living room, and pantry. Fresh water was supplied by rain collected from the roof and stored in 4000-gallon tanks in the cellar. In 1998 the Town of York took title to the light station.

Although Nubble Light has not been the site of many shipwrecks, the *Isadore* went aground just north of Nubble Point in 1842. All hands were lost, and it has been rumored that the ship is now a ghost ship. Some fishermen have reported seeing the ship sailing straight toward the cliffs, and then disappearing into the shadowy depths of Cape Neddick Bay.

The Nubble keeper witnessed another wreck on January 12, 1923. In blizzard conditions, the *Robert W*, suffering storm damage, became uncontrollable as it rounded the Nubble and the seventy-five foot schooner headed straight for Long Sands beach. Within a short time she ran aground, hard and fast, about three hundred yards offshore. Heavy seas poured over the decks. Captain Mitchell and his son, Stanley, had left Thomaston, Maine with a

Cape Neddick Light Station   *U.S. Coast Guard Photo*

load of boxboards and were heading for Lynn, Massachusetts. When the ship grounded she listed on the starboard side, taking the full brunt of the heavy sea. Sub-zero temperatures caused ice to build up on her rapidly. With life preservers tied around their waists, the Captain and his son each climbed up a mast and lashed themselves to the beams with heavy rope.

Herb Donnell, one of the first men on the scene, made a heroic but unsuccessful attempt to launch a small boat in the breaking surf. At about noon, word of the wreck reached town. Harry Bracy was in Garfield's Store at York Beach when the phone rang and Ada Stover, the telephone operator, reported the news.

Harry recalled watching Will Morton, a fisherman, and Ed Goodwin pull up their hip boots and start down the unplowed road. The snow was so high that both men had to pick up their legs and thrust them out sideways to make headway. It took almost an hour to get to the scene of the accident, about one mile away. Dr. Cook from York Village had been notified, and he and another rescue party were on their way. The men set up headquarters in Jimmy Lloyd's house, next to the old Hotel Mitchell.

At about two o'clock, Howard Kelly, on shore leave as second lighthouse keeper on Boon Island, spotted Frank Philbrick and the two men launched a sixteen foot rowboat they dragged down from the Vile's cottage. Rowing against the tide, they were beaten back by the thundering waves and blown away from the wreck by the powerful winds. They drifted down to the end of the beach before they could land. Frank had on a ten cent pair of cotton gloves and his hands were frozen. They made another attempt, and again the wind drove them away from the ship. It looked as if all was lost. Darkness had set in, mounds of ice were building up on the stranded *Robert W* and it was thought that the Captain and his son must be frozen to death.

The rescuers started a large fire on the beach to keep themselves warm and to give hope, if they could see it, to the men lashed to the masts. Professor Morse's son took a headlight from a car that was sitting in a winter storage garage and rigged it up to a battery so that a beam of light would be played on the ship. It was a sad and ghostly sight.

The Nubble Light Station had notified the Portsmouth Coast Guard Station which called in a boat from the Isles of Shoals equipped with a breeches buoy, a lifesaving device for bringing passengers ashore from a wrecked ship. However, this boat was of no use because the heavy seas kept it well offshore. At ten o'clock, Frank and Howard made another attempt to launch the rescue dory up the beach, figuring that this time they would be blown into the ship instead of by it. The strategy worked - a line was attached to the *Robert W* and the dory was secure.

Captain Mitchell cut his lifeline and slid to the deck, his hands and body badly frozen. Frank caught him around the legs and hauled him into the dory. Stanley fell from the mast and landed in the pounding sea. Frank jumped into the ocean and held onto the boy. The ice on Stanley, especially around the life preserver, kept both men floating. Frank claimed later that the water felt very warm to him, because the water temperature was so much warmer than the air.

The shore crew pulled and hauled the line attached to the dory and it slowly made its way back to shore. Frank and Stanley clung to the side of the dory and Howard and the Captain were inside. When the four men were pulled up on the beach, Frank and Stanley couldn't move - their clothes were instantly frozen stiff by the frigid wind. The four men were then lugged to Ed Mitchell's cottage, where Jimmy had a hot fire going and Dr. Cook gave everyone a shot of rum. After a couple of days of recuperation Captain Mitchell and his son returned to their home in Rockland. The *Robert W* broke up and her cargo washed ashore. A local man took charge of collecting the thousands of feet of lumber and hired a group of high school boys to work for a few cents per day to stack the boards until he could dispose of them. The site of the old wreck is marked by some rocks that divide the sandy beach. A mast salvaged from the *Robert W* was used as a flag pole in front of the York Harbor Reading Room - a monument to the "Downeasters" who braved the perilous sea.

Conclusion - The Lighthouse Legacy

The stories of the keepers and families who lived and worked at these beacons illustrate a devotion to duty, courage, strength and endurance beyond measure. The very structures themselves are examples of the human spirit - tested by time and nature, they stand on precarious ledges and on windy sea-swept granite islands as evidence of the brute force, determination and skillfull engineering needed to construct them. Today, some of these dignified structures are rusty and frayed, but their beacons still shine.

A legacy is a gift handed down from the past. Although the stories of lighthouses, keepers and shipwrecks are now whispers from another time, they are tales of the true patriots of the sea. They are honorable, filling our hearts with pride as we ponder our heritage, and inspirational as we face our own difficult challenges. They are the lighthouse legacies.

Bill Thomson is a native New Englander, residing in Kennebunk, Maine. He retired in 1996, Professor Emiritus, after teaching for thirty-three years in the History Department at Salem State College, Salem, Massachusetts. Throughout his career he has written twenty-two books and produced several documentaries which have been shown on New England television channels. He has appeared nationally on PBS, The Learning Channel and The Discovery Channel. He lectures and volunteers at local schools, civic groups and churches. His writings reflect interesting incidents and amazing anecdotes which illustrate the human interest side of history.

Cape Porpoise   *Oil Painting by Ron Goyette*

Ron Goyette has maintained a studio in Kennebunkport, Maine for over thirty years. His paintings are in private and public collections in seven countries. His limited edition lithographs can be found in over fifty galleries throughout New England. His work captures the essence of nostalgic turn-of-the-century life in New England.

Bibliography

"Editor's Easy Chair." (1869, June) Harper's New Monthly Magazine, p.141.
http://cdl.library.cornell.edu/cgi-bin/moa/moa-cgi?notisid=ABK4014-0039-20

Finnegan, Kathleen and Timothy E. Harrison. "Lighthouses of Maine and New Hampshire." Wells, ME: Lighthouse Digest, Inc., 1991.

Kabbe, Gustav. "Heroism In The Lighthouse Service. A Description of Life On Matinicus Rock." (1897, June) The Century; A Popular Quarterly, pp. 219-231.
http://cdl.library.cornell.edu/cgi-bin/moa/moa-cgi?notisid=ABP2287-0054-45

Small, Constance Scovill. "The Lighthouse Keeper's Wife." Orono, ME: The University Press, 1986.

Snow, Edward Rowe. "Famous Lighthouses of New England." Boston, MA: Yankee Publishing Co., 1945.

Snow, Edward Rowe. "The Lighthouses of New England." New York: Dodd, Mead & Co., 1973.

Sterling, Robert T. "Lighthouses of the Maine Coast and the Men Who Keep Them." Brattleboro, VT: Stephen Daye Press, 1935.

Thompson, Courtney. "Maine Lighthouses, A Pictorial Guide." Mt. Desert, ME: Cat Nap Publications, 1996.

Thomson, William O. "Solitary Vigils At Boon Island Light." Kennebunk, ME: 'Scapes Me, 2000.

United States Coast Guard: http://www.uscg.mil/hq/g-cp/history/collect.html

United States Navy: http://www.history.navy.mil/wars/revwar/officers.htm

United States Navy: http://www.ussconstitution.navy.mil/